THE S. S. HUEBNER FOUNDATION FOR INSURANCE EDUCATION

Lectures

LIFE INSURANCE TRENDS AND PROBLEMS
LIFE INSURANCE TRENDS AT MID-CENTURY
INVESTMENT OF LIFE INSURANCE FUNDS
ACCIDENT AND SICKNESS INSURANCE
PENSIONS: PROBLEMS AND TRENDS
THE BENEFICIARY IN LIFE INSURANCE
LIFE INSURANCE SALES MANAGEMENT
ALL LINES INSURANCE

Studies

AN ANALYSIS OF GOVERNMENT LIFE INSURANCE
THE ECONOMIC THEORY OF RISK AND INSURANCE
GROUP ANNUITIES
LIFE INSURANCE HOUSING PROJECTS
LIFE INSURANCE INVESTMENT IN COMMERCIAL REAL ESTATE
TOTAL DISABILITY PROVISIONS IN LIFE INSURANCE CONTRACTS
INSURANCE AND ECONOMIC THEORY
GROUP LIFE INSURANCE
COMPULSORY TEMPORARY DISABILITY INSURANCE IN THE
    UNITED STATES
TRANSITION TO MULTIPLE-LINE INSURANCE COMPANIES
GROUP HEALTH INSURANCE

GROUP HEALTH INSURANCE

By

JESSE F. PICKRELL, PH.D., C.L.U., C.P.C.U.
Professor of Insurance
North Texas State University

Revised Edition

Published for
THE S. S. HUEBNER FOUNDATION
FOR INSURANCE EDUCATION
University of Pennsylvania

by

RICHARD D. IRWIN, INC., Homewood, Illinois

THE S. S. HUEBNER FOUNDATION
FOR INSURANCE EDUCATION

The S. S. Huebner Foundation for Insurance Education was created in 1940, under the sponsorship of the American Life Convention, the Life Insurance Association of America (then the Association of Life Insurance Presidents), and the Institute of Life Insurance, and operated under a deed of trust until 1955 at which time it was incorporated as a Pennsylvania nonprofit corporation. Its primary purpose is to strengthen and encourage education at the collegiate level. Its activities take three principal forms:

a) The providing of fellowships and scholarships to teachers in accredited colleges and universities of the United States and Canada, or persons who are contemplating a teaching career in such colleges and universities, in order that they may secure preparation at the graduate level for insurance teaching and research.

b) The publication of research theses and other studies which constitute a distinct contribution directly or indirectly to insurance knowledge.

c) The collection and maintenance of an insurance library and other research materials which are made available through circulating privileges to teachers in accredited colleges and universities desirous of conducting research in the insurance field.

Financial support for the Foundation is provided by contributions from more than one hundred life insurance companies and proceeds from the sale of Foundation publications.

The program of activities is under the general direction of a Board of Trustees representing the life insurance institution. Actual operation of the Foundation has been delegated to the University of Pennsylvania under an administrative plan submitted by the University and approved by the Board of Trustees. The University discharges its responsibilities through an Administrative Board consisting of six officers and faculty members of the University of Pennsylvania and three faculty members of other universities. Active management of the Foundation is entrusted to an Executive Director, appointed by the University of Pennsylvania.

vii

FOREWORD

THIS is a revision of a volume which was originally published as a doctoral dissertation under the title of *Group Disability Insurance*. Its publication completed a trilogy of books pertaining to the three broad areas of group operations, the other two volumes being *Group Life Insurance* by Davis W. Gregg, and *Group Annuities* by Kenneth Black, Jr. Through their use for educational purposes, these volumes have made a signal contribution to an understanding and appreciation of the group insurance mechanism. The dynamic nature of group insurance has already necessitated a revision of *Group Life Insurance* and is responsible for this particular revision.

Group health insurance is an especially dynamic sector of the insurance field, which required the inclusion of much new material in the revised edition. At the same time that the book was being updated, it was reorganized in an attempt to maximize its value as an educational tool. New topics were added, some old topics were expanded, and some of the original material was deleted altogether. As was true of the original volume, the revised edition benefitted from the criticism and suggestions of a number of experts in the group health insurance field. The Foundation is very much indebted to those persons—identified in the author's preface—for their valuable and generous assistance.

A native of Texas, Dr. Pickrell received both the B.S. and M.B.A. degrees from North Texas State University, the former in 1946 and the latter in 1948. At the conclusion of his work at North Texas State, he was awarded a Huebner Foundation fellowship and studied at the University of Pennsylvania for the next three years. He returned to North Texas State in the fall of 1951 as an Associate Professor of Insurance and continued to work on his dissertation. Upon receiving his Ph.D. degree in 1956, he was promoted to the rank of Professor of Insurance at North Texas State University, a position which he still holds. He also serves as Chairman of the Department of Insurance at that institution.

The Foundation wishes to express its profound gratitude to Dr. Pickrell for undertaking the revision of his book under the most trying personal circumstances. The Executive Director also wishes to record his gratification at the manner in which the task was carried out.

The nature of the purposes for which the Foundation was created precludes it from taking an editorial position on controversial insurance theories or practices. It does not, therefore, detract in any wise from the quality of this volume to state that the findings of fact and conclusions derived therefrom are those of the author and not of the Foundation.

DAN M. MCGILL
Executive Director

Philadelphia
October, 1961

PREFACE

GROUP health insurance has shown remarkable growth since the inception of the first group medical care cover just over three decades ago. Most of the growth occurred during and after World War II, and premiums paid to private and association carriers for this type of insurance increased from $369 million in 1945 to $5,060 million in 1959.

This book represents a complete revision of the volume published in 1958 under the title *Group Disability Insurance.* The material has been brought up to date and reorganized substantially. It would be impractical to attempt to cover in a single volume all the details and problems of group health insurance; details, problems, and practices change constantly. This volume is intended as a comprehensive source of information on the broad outlines of group health insurance principles and practices.

It is impossible to acknowledge the cooperation and help of all company executives and group insurance personnel who have had a part in the preparation of the original volume or of this revision. The original volume was prepared under the direct supervision of the late Dr. C. Arthur Kulp, who at the time of his death was Dean of the Wharton School of Finance and Commerce at the University of Pennsylvania. The assistance and inspiration of this brilliant and beloved scholar contributed greatly to the completion of the original study. As Executive Director of the S. S. Huebner Foundation for Insurance Education during the period of the author's residence at the University of Pennsylvania, the late Dr. David McCahan exerted a strong influence on the original study. Dr. Dan M. McGill, the present Executive Director of the Foundation, offered many valuable suggestions concerning reorganization and scope of the material in the revised volume.

Special recognition should be accorded to Paul Rinker, Vice President of Continental Assurance Company, Charles E. Probst, Vice President, Group Division, of the Provident Mutual Life Insurance Company, and Morton D. Miller, Vice President and Associate Actuary of the Equitable Life Assurance Society of the United States. These three were of great assistance in reading the entire manuscript and offering many valuable suggestions for its improvement. It should go without saying that no one who read the manuscript during its preparation is responsible for errors or shortcomings in the completed volume.

Thanks are due G. Victor Hallman, Director of Educational Publications of the American College of Life Underwriters, for his assistance in getting the revised manuscript typed. Much credit must go to Mildred A. Brill for her able handling of the many details incident to publication of the manuscript.

The greatest debt of all is owed to my wife. Her constant inspiration and encouragement made both the original and revised versions seem a necessity. Her expert handling of the many problems centered around four wonderfully normal children made the revision possible.

J. F. P.

Denton, Texas
September, 1961

TABLE OF CONTENTS

LIST OF TABLES

CHAPTER I

THE BASIC NATURE OF GROUP HEALTH INSURANCE

GROUP insurance in general may be described as one of the two private mechanisms for insuring against the disability hazard, the other being individual insurance. The selection of lives to be insured by group insurance is on the basis of groups of persons, and not by individual lives as is the case in individual insurance.

The group insurance field includes not only health insurance, but group life insurance and group annuities as well. In this book, references to the problems and practices in the life and annuity fields will be made only for purposes of comparison or clarification.

Many of the underwriting, administrative, and rating details of group health insurance can be overlooked initially in examining the fundamentals of this field of insurance. In this chapter the basic nature of group health insurance will be discussed under the general headings of characteristics and legal definitions by the various states. The final section of the chapter will be devoted to a discussion of the growth and scope of the group health insurance field.

CHARACTERISTICS OF GROUP HEALTH INSURANCE

Whether it be group life insurance, group annuities, or group health insurance, there are several fundamental characteristics essential for the successful operation of a group insurance plan. Some of these fundamental characteristics apply, of course, to insurance in general, and by themselves would not set group insurance apart from individual insurance. Others apply only to group insurance because of the different methods by which underwriting objectives are attained.[1]

Three-Party Insurance

Group insurance contracts are issued to employers, unions, associations, or trustees, but the contract is made for the benefit of someone other than the policyholder. The individuals (and their families) protected by the insurance are not parties to the group contract. A given group contract over a period will provide insurance for a constantly changing group of individuals without any disturbance to the basic contract. Insurance for new group members is provided as they qualify, and coverage for others is terminated as they leave the group.

Types of Groups Eligible for Insurance

A group of people can be eligible for group insurance only if a single, mutual interest other than insurance binds them together. This mutual interest should be so strong that the advantages or disadvantages of joining or leaving the group will not materially be offset or affected by the presence of group insurance. Underwriting rules vary by company, but in general the following types of policyholders are eligible for group health insurance:

1. Employers or trustees of a fund established by an employer.
2. An association or union.
3. Trustees of a fund established by one or more labor unions.
4. Trustees of a fund established by two or more employers in the same industry.
5. Trustees of a fund established jointly by union and employers or by an association.
6. Other types of groups (such as public bodies) not prohibited by state law or ruling.[2]

---

[1] For an excellent discussion of the fundamentals of group insurance, see G. W. Fitzhugh, "Group Life and Disability Insurance on the One-Year Term Premium Basis," *Transactions of the Actuarial Society of America*, Vol. 46 (1945), pp. 239 ff.

[2] See page 5 for a discussion of state laws and rulings.

Insurance without Individual Selection

In personal or individual insurance against disability, the insurance company may accept or decline an individual applicant on the basis of his personal habits, the condition of his health, medical history, age, income, or any other factors that appear pertinent to the risk acceptance. Although such selection is available to the group underwriter under some state laws, individual underwriting is seldom used except perhaps in groups involving only five or ten lives. Group underwriting, then, is concerned primarily with the group as a whole and not the individuals within the group. Selection against the company is of course a problem in any form of insurance, so the group health plan must somehow preclude excessive individual selection.

Prevention of Adverse Selection

It is almost a foregone conclusion that no insurance company could write a group plan at a premium rate that would be acceptable to the group if the "unhealthy" or "accident-prone" members of the group could elect the insurance freely and the healthier members could elect to leave or remain out of the group insured. However, restrictions upon freedom to elect the insurance are not enough to protect the insurance company against adverse selection. Restrictions must also be placed upon freedom to elect types and amounts of benefits, since the results of this type of selection could be just as serious as those of election in or out of the insurance plan.

The insurance company secures a spread of risk, which otherwise would have to be secured entirely by individual underwriting, by requiring a minimum number of employees, participation of a minimum percentage of eligible employees, and individual underwriting for delayed application or reinstatement. In addition, each insured member of a given group will be insured automatically for the types and amounts of benefits applicable to his particular employee "class."

Underwriting rules vary by company and by state, and the

minimum number for an employer group may be two, five, ten, or twenty-five employees. When employees pay all or part of the costs of insurance, the general rule is that at least 75 per cent of the eligible employees must be insured under the plan, with the class or classes of eligible employees determined by conditions pertaining to employment. If the employer pays all the premiums, all eligible employees must be insured under the insurance plan, with eligibility determined by conditions pertaining to employment.

Simplicity and Economy of Administration

A group health insurance plan should be simple in its operation. Simplicity is essential not only to secure economy of operation, but also to promote good will toward the insurance company and the employer. Certificates of insurance issued to employees must outline benefits clearly to avoid misunderstandings and possible abuse, and to acquaint the certificate holder with his rights under the master contract.

A group plan should have full employer co-operation in installation and administration. Promotion and selling efforts can and must be concentrated on the employer, and the employer can in turn use his influence to interest the employees in the insurance. The assumption of many of the administrative functions by the employer results in a very low administrative cost to the insurance company. Collection of the employee's contribution (if any) toward the premiums can usually be accomplished by payroll deductions, and a single premium remittance can be made by the policyholder, thus obviating perhaps thousands of premium notices and individual premium collections. Some of the larger groups are permitted to administer their own claims, issue certificates to individual employees, and prepare their own monthly premium statements.

There are several reasons why employer contributions to premium payments are usually considered essential to success of group insurance plans:

1. Substantial employer contribution assures the active employer interest and co-operation so essential to successful administration of a group plan.

2. The employer contribution makes for better relations with his employees, since frequent contacts with employees make the contributions appear to be an extra benefit of a personal nature.

3. Premium refunds or dividends may become a problem in future years unless the employer contribution is large enough that the employer is legally entitled to receive and retain the entire dividend. It becomes a serious problem to distribute premium refunds among employees, which would be necessary under an employee-pay-all arrangement.

4. An employer contribution can be increased to absorb any renewal premium rate increases that may become necessary in future years. Otherwise, it would be necessary to re-enroll employees individually each time premium rates were raised. A re-enrollment required by a small increase in premium might cause a great deal of employee dissatisfaction.

5. Employer contributions make it possible to keep costs to employees low enough to attract the better risks and at the same time cover the poorer risks.

LEGAL DEFINITIONS OF GROUP HEALTH INSURANCE

In 1940, in its Model Group Accident and Health Insurance Bill,[3] the National Association of Insurance Commissioners recommended for adoption in the states a definition of group health insurance. The bill contained a definition of the types of groups eligible for insurance, the minimum number of certificate holders required for each type of group, and minimum participation percentages for both contributory and noncontributory groups.

In the model bill the minimum of certificate holders for all groups was set forth as twenty-five. For noncontributory groups (that is, where the employee or certificate holder contributes nothing to the cost of insurance), all eligible employees had to be insured; and under contributory groups the model

[3] National Association of Insurance Commissioners, *Proceedings,* 1940, pp. 56–60.

bill required participation of at least 75 per cent of all eligible employees. The bill required that the class or classes of eligible employees must be determined by conditions pertaining to employment.

No state has adopted the 1940 model bill in its entirety, although a number of states have followed it to some extent in their laws and rulings. In 1948 the Health and Accident Underwriters Conference prepared a different type of model bill. The Conference bill was revised on November 6, 1950, and again on March 1, 1954.

The revised Conference bill departed from the 1940 model bill in a number of respects:

1. The minimum number of lives required for employer groups was reduced from twenty-five to ten.

2. The minimum number remained twenty-five for policies issued with associations or unions as policyholders, but no minimum was specified for group policies issued to trustees of a fund established by two or more employers in the same industry or by one or more labor unions or by both.

3. The Conference bill clearly specified that eligible persons may be insured with or without members of their families or dependents—thus the dependent or family member is not insured, but the employee is insured against health losses resulting from the hospital, surgical, or medical expenses of dependents.

4. No minimum participation requirements were set forth in the Conference bill.

The 1940 model bill, in requiring minimum participation of 75 per cent, was actually prescribing an underwriting rule which perhaps should be a function of company group underwriting. Some states that do prescribe minimum percentage requirements have recognized this to some extent by reducing the percentage below seventy-five.

On October 4, 1957, the Health Insurance Association of America, successor association to the Conference, announced a revised model bill recommended for adoption by the various states. The principal change in the HIAA bill from the 1954 Conference bill was the removal of all minimum size requirements for employer, association, or union groups. Under this latest model bill, the establishment of minimum size requirements would be left up to individual companies. Other changes made by the 1957 model bill were largely editorial, but there was some broadening of the definitions of employees eligible under some types of groups.[4]

The model bill definitions of group health insurance have been followed in some states, but for all practical purposes the states may be divided into three broad groups: (1) sixteen states and the District of Columbia have no group health law or ruling; (2) sixteen states have a law or ruling which defines group health insurance and prescribes minimum percentage requirements; and (3) eighteen states have a law or ruling which defines group health insurance but does not prescribe minimum percentage requirements.[5]

In states without a law or ruling, group companies set their own rules as to types of groups to be written, minimum group size, and minimum percentage requirements. In the other states, insurance may be written to cover any kind of group specifically permitted or not prohibited by the particular law or ruling. Of the thirty-four states with a group law or ruling, six prescribe no minimum group size, four require a minimum group of two, seven require a minimum group of five, sixteen require a minimum group of ten, and one requires a minimum group of fifteen.

SCOPE OF GROUP HEALTH INSURANCE

Group health insurance has undergone remarkable growth in the years since the addition, in 1938, of hospital expense insurance for dependents and surgical expense insurance for employees and dependents. Part of this growth could have been expected to result from a general expansion of economic activity and higher incomes, but a large portion can probably be attributed to an ever-increasing recognition of the value of

---

[4] See Appendix A for a copy of the HIAA bill.
[5] See Appendix B for a summary of state laws and rulings in effect in January, 1961.

group insurance in meeting and distributing losses due to the disability hazard. This recognition was no doubt substantially increased during the World War II "wage freeze" period when fringe benefits such as group health insurance were not subject to the freeze. The recognition of the advantages of group insurance has been evidenced most clearly in the attitudes of employees in general, and unions in particular, that group insurance is an important part of any contract of employment. In 1940 total premiums paid for health insurance of all kinds in the United States totaled $300 million, and this represented only 0.4 per cent of disposable personal income for the year. In 1959 total premiums paid had increased to $6.7 billion, which represented 2 per cent of disposable personal income in the United States.[6]

Group Insurance Premium Volume

The figures cited above include premiums for individual insurance, but Table 1 shows the growth in group insurance premiums from 1945 to 1959.

The tremendous increase in group health premium volume is readily apparent from an examination of Table 1. It is also apparent that private insurers and the Blue Cross types of plans have had approximately equal shares of the income throughout this period.

Part of the increase during the period shown in Table 1 was caused by a rise in the level of benefits to employees and dependents, in step with higher wages and costs of medical care; but probably a larger portion was due to the increase in the number of persons covered.

Individuals Covered

The extent of the development of the entire health insurance field probably can best be shown by a breakdown of the entire field into the number of persons covered in the five

---

[6] Health Insurance Institute, *Source Book of Health Insurance Data*, 1960, p. 31.

TABLE 1

TOTAL PREMIUMS FOR GROUP HEALTH INSURANCE
IN THE UNITED STATES, 1945–59
(000,000 Omitted)

Year	Insurance Companies	Blue Cross, Blue Shield, and Similar Plans	Total
1959	$2,560	$2,500	$5,060
1958	2,310	2,184	4,494
1957	2,160	1,969	4,129
1956	1,850	1,785	3,635
1955	1,573	1,523	3,096
1954	1,382	1,367	2,749
1953	1,239	1,224	2,463
1952	1,022	1,036	2,058
1951	853	863	1,716
1950	629	687	1,316
1949	460	555	1,015
1948	386	385	771
1947	306	297	603
1946	229	195	424
1945	215	154	369

Source: Health Insurance Institute, *Source Book of Health Insurance Data*, 1960, pp. 28, 30.

main sublines of insurance. Table 2 shows the number of individuals in the United States covered for the years 1945–59. Duplications in coverage have been eliminated from the figures shown in Table 2.

All of the forms of insurance in Table 2 have shown an annual increase in the number of persons covered throughout the period included, with two minor exceptions in coverage for loss of income. Although they show consistent annual increases, the rate of increase in the basic medical reimbursement types of coverage has declined in recent years. This decline in the rate of increase is due at least in part to the fact that so large a proportion of the population now has voluntary insurance. The decline is due also in part to the rapid rate of increase in the major medical types of coverage.

Health Insurance Benefits

A record of $5.2 billion in health insurance benefits was paid to insured persons by all types of voluntary insuring

TABLE 2

NUMBER OF PEOPLE WITH HEALTH INSURANCE PROTECTION
IN THE UNITED STATES, BY TYPE OF COVERAGE
1945–1959
(000 Omitted)

End of Year	Hospital Expense	Surgical Expense	Regular Medical Expense	Major Medical Expense*	Loss of Income †
1959	127,896	116,944	82,615	21,850	43,169
1958	123,038	111,435	75,395	17,375	41,870
1957	121,432	108,931	71,813	13,262	42,939
1956	115,949	101,325	64,891	8,876	41,688
1955	107,662	91,927	55,506	5,241	39,513
1954	101,493	85,890	47,248	2,198	39,397
1953	97,303	80,982	42,684	1,220	39,571
1952	90,965	72,459	35,670	689	38,373
1951	85,348	64,892	27,723	108	38,035
1950	76,639	54,156	21,589	—	37,793
1949	66,044	41,143	16,862	—	33,626
1948	60,995	34,060	12,895	—	32,700
1947	52,584	26,247	8,898	—	30,574
1946	42,112	18,609	6,421	—	26,229
1945	32,068	12,890	4,713	—	—

Source: Health Insurance Institute, *Source Book of Health Insurance Data*, 1960, p. 11.
  * Major medical expense figures are for insurance companies only and do not include such plans provided by Blue Cross, Blue Shield, medical societies, or independent organizations.
  † Loss of income figures include formal paid sick leave plans and coverage provided through employee organizations.

organizations during 1959.[7] This total represented a 90 per cent increase over the amount of benefits paid in 1954, and over five times the benefit total ten years earlier. The $5.2 billion of total benefits in 1959 was made up of $838 million of income reimbursement and $4.34 billion of medical expense reimbursement.

The U.S. Department of Commerce and the U.S. Department of Health, Education, and Welfare estimate that in the United States during 1959 total expenditures for medical care were $18.3 billion, of which voluntary insurance paid less than one fourth.[8] There are, however, many reasons why the disparity between voluntary insurance benefits and total expenditures does not prove that voluntary insurance is inadequate.

[7] *Ibid.*, p. 36.
[8] *Ibid.*, p. 53.

First, the uninsured segment of total population in the United States includes recipients of public assistance, a certain number of veterans, other individuals with some public resources for medical care available to them, and an unknown number of persons of such economic status that they may not feel the need for insurance.[9] Expenditures for medical care by those who do not feel the need for insurance are probably much higher than average because of the quantity and types of medical services used, and this produces a further distortion of "uninsured" medical expenses.

A second reason why voluntary insurance does not cover all medical expenditures is that not all medical expenditures are insurable on a voluntary or any other basis. Included in the $18.2 billion total expenditures in 1959 are $4.8 billion for medicines and appliances, $2 billion for dental care, and $1.1 billion for miscellaneous services.[10] Some unknown portion of this $7.7 billion total would of course be insurable, but items not insurable would include such things as eye examinations and glasses, nonprescription drugs and medicines, luxury hospital accommodations, and at least some portion of dental care.

A third reason why voluntary insurance does not cover all expenditures involves the approaches which have been taken to expense reimbursement insurance. Historically, this type of insurance has included a substantial degree of "first-dollar" coverage of small medical expenses which can better be budgeted out of current income. However, the trend toward major medical coverage by both private and association carriers indicates that voluntary insurance is moving in the direction of insuring the portion of total expenditures that can best be insured.

---

[9] Report of the Committee on Labor and Public Welfare, United States Senate, "Health Insurance Plans in the United States," May 28, 1951, pp. 2–3.

[10] Health Insurance Institute, *op. cit.*, p. 53.

CHAPTER II

TYPES OF GROUP HEALTH INSURANCE

THERE is no standard group health policy issued in this country, but the policy provisions for group health insurance vary only slightly among the companies. In analyzing these contracts, it would be fruitless and unnecessary to attempt to point out differences in wording and organization of the contracts among different companies. Consequently, the policy forms of one large company will be discussed in detail as representing typical contracts of all companies, with consideration given to existing major variations.

A single master contract issued to an employer may provide all of the group health covers: income reimbursement, hospital expense, surgical expense, all forms of medical expense, and accidental death and dismemberment. Some of the covers may be issued alone or in various combinations.[1] In view of the many different arrangements the master contract may follow, it seems advisable to discuss the provisions under two major divisions: (1) those provisions peculiar to specific insurance covers, and (2) those provisions common to all covers regardless of the combinations comprising any particular master contract. This chapter includes all those provisions peculiar to specific insurance covers except those dealing primarily with the certificate and rights of the certificate holder, which will be included in Chapter III. Other contract provisions common to all covers are discussed in Chapter III, and these include provisions relating to employee eligibility for coverage, definitions, and duties of the insurer and the policyholder.

---

[1] See Chapter III.

12

Many of the provisions in a master contract appear only if the master contract covers the particular economic loss to which the provision applies. For each type of loss covered there must be an insuring clause, a description of the benefits, and a description of the limitations or exclusions applicable. Accordingly, the provisions in this chapter will be grouped under the two principal kinds of group health insurance which may be written: income reimbursement insurance and expense reimbursement insurance. Income reimbursement insurance includes coverage for both temporary and longer term loss of income through disability, and the accidental death and dismemberment cover. Group expense reimbursement insurance includes all the forms of group insurance which provide benefits to cover all or part of medical care costs.

INCOME REIMBURSEMENT INSURANCE

Short-Term Income Reimbursement Insurance

Insuring Clause. The insuring agreement is that part of an insurance contract which states the insurance company's promise to pay benefits. A widely used insuring clause for short-term benefits reads as follows:

If any employee while insured for Income Reimbursement Insurance under this policy becomes wholly and continuously disabled by:

(1) An accidental bodily injury which does not arise out of and in the course of any employment for wage or profit, or

(2) Disease for which the employee is not entitled to a benefit under any Workmen's Compensation Law or Act, and is prevented from performing any and every duty of his occupation, a weekly benefit is payable to the employee in an amount determined in accordance with the provision entitled "Amounts of Insurance" contained herein for the period of such disability but not exceeding *twenty-six* weeks during any one period of disability, whether from one or more causes, and no benefit shall be payable for the first *seven* days of any disability *due to disease.*

Successive periods of disability separated by less than *two* weeks of active work on full time shall be considered one period of disability unless the subsequent disability is due to an injury or disease entirely unrelated to the causes of the previous disability and commences after the employee has returned to active work on full time.

In the event of disability caused by a pregnancy, which term includes resulting childbirth or miscarriage, weekly benefits shall be payable for not more than six weeks for all disability resulting from any one pregnancy.

This insuring clause establishes three major provisions in connection with the insurance:

1. The causes or origins of disability for which benefits are payable.
2. The results or definition of disability which makes an employee eligible for benefits.
3. A reference to a description of benefits and limitations here and elsewhere in the contract.

The causes of disability are briefly and broadly defined: nonoccupational sickness or nonoccupational accidental bodily injury.[2]

In the clause cited above, accidents are excluded if they "arise out of *and* in the course of employment," but a provision sometimes used excludes accidents "arising out of *or* in the course of employment." In the latter, accidents are excluded if either condition is met, and this results in a narrow twilight zone of accidents which satisfy one condition but not both and are thus ineligible for payment under either workmen's compensation or group insurance. The principal examples of cases of this type are accidents resulting from drunkenness on the job or direct disobedience of orders.

The definition of the result of the accidental bodily injuries or sickness required to make an employee eligible for benefits is that he be "wholly and continuously disabled," and "prevented from performing any and every duty of his occupation." The interpretation of these provisions is more im-

---

[2] Former geographical restrictions and exclusion of self-inflicted injuries are disappearing, but the claimant is still required to be under treatment by or under the care of a legally qualified physician. However, the term "physician" may mean any person who treats human ailments, and the restrictions imposed by "legally qualified" vary from state to state. To provide a uniform basis of administration in all lines of group health insurance, some companies use the less liberal term "legally qualified doctor of medicine." See discussion by Wendell A. Milliman, *Record of the American Institute of Actuaries,* Vol. 34 (1945), p. 310.

portant in long-term income reimbursement insurance, where benefits may extend for the whole life, and where a distinction may be made between total and partial disability. The problem is not so serious in short-term insurance, where benefits are limited to ten, thirteen, or twenty-six weeks, and seldom more than fifty-two weeks, and where the benefit level for the individual claimant has been set substantially below his earnings. The practical test of an eligible claim in group short-term insurance is whether an otherwise employable worker is unable to work. However, the insurer does reserve the right to examine the claimant at reasonable times and does require that he be under the direct care of a physician. Otherwise, there would be no way to control malingering.

Benefits.   The insuring clause states the period for which benefits will be paid to an employee. This provision varies in wording among different insurance companies, but whatever its form, it imposes three essential limitations:

1. The waiting period applicable to accidental bodily injuries and sickness.
2. The maximum period for which benefits are payable for any one continuous period of disability.
3. Special maximum periods for specified causes of disability.

Waiting Period.   Income benefits for a disabled employee may begin on the first day of his disability, or they may begin at some later time specified in the insurance contract. The use of a waiting period is an application of the deductible principle to the group accident and sickness cover. Sometimes called an "elimination period," the waiting period eliminates weekly income payments for the initial period of any disability. For example, if the waiting period provided in the contract is seven days for disability due to accident and sickness, weekly income benefits to a disabled employee begin on the eighth day of disability.

The waiting period provision for a particular group may specify that the same waiting period applies whether the disability is due to accident or sickness, or the contract may provide no waiting period for disability due to accident but provide a waiting period for disability due to sickness. The usual waiting period applicable to disability due to sickness is seven days, with income benefits to begin on the eighth day of disability. The waiting period for sickness generally is not longer than fourteen days, and three days is the shortest waiting period ever applied to a group. The waiting period for accidents is never longer in any particular policy than that for sickness, and group plans very commonly pay benefits from the first day for disabilities due to accident.

The use of the waiting period is easily justified. For both accident and sickness the elimination of small budgetable losses reduces the cost of insurance by reducing both the pure premium necessary to pay losses and the administrative expense. Even stronger reasons justify its use for the sickness hazard; malingering is always a possibility, because sickness is more easily feigned than accident. Sickness disability is much more difficult to define or measure, even by the claimant himself; and finally, when benefits are payable immediately, "a few days rest" for the least significant illness could appear attractive even to honest claimants.

Maximum Period of Benefits.   The period of benefit payment for any one continuous disability is limited to a specified maximum number of weeks. Thirteen weeks is the maximum period most commonly provided, but short-term disability contracts may be written providing ten, twenty-six, or for select groups, fifty-two or more weeks of benefit for any one period of continuous disability. The benefit period begins on the day following the end of the applicable waiting period and runs to the end of the maximum period provided in the contract, or to the prior termination of the disability.

Special Maternity Provision.   Special provision is made in the contract for maternity benefits, if maternity coverage applies. For disability caused by any one pregnancy and resulting childbirth, abortion, or miscarriage, benefits are usually limited to a maximum period of six weeks. This limitation is necessary because longer periods away from work are usually for homemaking purposes and not due to disability. Maternity benefits are limited to pregnancies which terminate after a specified period of coverage or which have their inception after the effective date of the insurance, but pre-existing pregnancies are usually covered for employees insured during initial enrollment for a group plan.

Age Restrictions.   Older employees may have only limited benefits when a disability is due to sickness, although age restrictions are tending to disappear due to union interest in such plans and the increasing tendency for workers to retire at age sixty-five rather than continue working. Some group plans limit the period of payment for a sickness disability commencing after age sixty to a specified maximum number of weeks in any one twelve-month period, rather than allow the full benefit period to be available for each separate disability.

Successive Periods of Disability.   The provision concerning successive periods of disability may work in favor of either the insurer or the claimant. The contract provides that successive periods of disability are considered as one, unless separated by two weeks of continuous active employment with the employer, or unless they arise from different or unrelated causes. In favor of the insurer, this provision serves to deter a claimant from returning to work for a few days to become eligible for another full period of benefit payment. A claimant who suffers two or more relatively short periods of disability from the same cause may be benefited by the provision inasmuch as a waiting period provision will be applied only to the first disability period.

Group Choice of Benefits.   The choice of waiting period and maximum benefit period is made by the group, not by individual employees. That is, different periods may be provided for different groups, but both the waiting period and the maximum benefit period are uniform for all employees within any given group.

Amount of Insurance.   The amount of weekly indemnity for which each employee is insured is determined by some plan precluding individual selection by the employees. In most groups it has been found that the most desirable plan of insurance establishes fixed insurance amounts for all employees in the same salary grouping.

Length of service or position are sometimes employed in group insurance as criteria for determining the amount of insurance, especially if earnings fluctuate—as might be the case with employees paid on a commission basis. A flat amount of insurance for each employee is frequently used under insurance plans arranged as the result of collective bargaining.

An example is given below of insurance benefits graded according to earnings classification:

Basic Weekly Earnings	Weekly Insurance Benefits
Less than $40	$20
$40 but less than $50	25
$50 but less than $60	30
$60 but less than $70	35
$70 and over	40

Since net take-home pay is considerably lower than gross pay, the general principle followed in such a plan is that the amount of weekly income reimbursement in each wage class should be from one half to two thirds of the usual weekly base pay for the class, excluding overtime pay or bonuses. The actual wage distribution is taken into consideration in establishing the wage classes. Once the classes are established, the amount of insurance provided for each employee on the effective date of his insurance is determined by the earnings table on the basis of his usual compensation during some predetermined base period.

There is no fixed maximum amount of benefit which companies are willing to write. Most companies grant higher maximum amounts to larger groups when a sufficient spread of risk can be secured.

Long-Term Income Reimbursement Insurance

Insurance against income loss for long periods is in its early experimental stage, so there is not much uniformity of coverage patterns, although the general principles discussed above apply to the longer term coverage.

Benefit periods may be limited to one year, two years, five

years, or to age sixty-five, although some plans pay benefits for life for disability due to accident. For longer benefit durations it is customary to require after the first or second year that the claimant be so disabled that he cannot engage in "any occupation for substantial gain or profit." With this type of provision, the test for an eligible claim becomes more strict after the initial period during which the claimant is entitled to benefits if unable to engage in "his occupation." Disabilities for the same cause and not separated by return to active work for at least three months are considered part of the same claim.

In general, coverage is both occupational and nonoccupational, although many plans reduce benefits by the amounts payable under workmen's compensation. Many plans also reduce benefits by the amounts payable under the disability coverage of the Federal Old Age, Survivors, and Disability program.

Waiting periods are generally substantially longer than those provided under the more common short-term disability income coverage. They may be set at 15, 30, 60, 90, or 180 days, and the usual practice is to set the waiting period so that benefits will start at the termination of short-term benefits or the employer's salary continuation plan.

Accidental Death and Dismemberment Insurance

Group insurance for accidental death and dismemberment is ordinarily written only in conjunction with some other group insurance cover. When issued with other income reimbursement coverage or with expense reimbursement coverage, it supplements the benefits provided under such insurance with principal sum benefits similar to those in individual personal health insurance.

There is no accurate method of determining the extent of the economic loss occasioned by death or dismemberment, so it is generally assumed that this form of insurance is a special type of income reimbursement coverage. Since most persons are probably underinsured against the hazards of death and dismemberment, this form of coverage is not considered a serious duplication of benefits available from some other form of insurance, as long as benefits are kept at a reasonable level. This insurance can thus be written to provide coverage for both occupational and nonoccupational causes, but it is frequently written on a nonoccupational basis for groups in more hazardous industries.

Insuring Clause.   Accidental death and dismemberment insurance provides exactly the protection its name implies, but only within the meaning of its rather restrictive insuring clause. A typical insuring clause is reproduced below:

If any employee, while insured for Accidental Death and Dismemberment Insurance under this Group Policy as a result of accidental bodily injuries, shall suffer, directly and independently of all other causes and within ninety days from the date of such injuries, any of the losses described below the Company shall pay the amount specified for such loss in the following Schedule: . . .

This insuring clause deals primarily with the causes required to establish a loss for which benefits are payable, but reference is made to a definition of the required results as well. The causes of loss for which coverage is provided are *accidental bodily injuries.* The bodily injuries must result in a scheduled loss (death or dismemberment) within ninety days and *directly and independently of all other causes.* The purpose of the phrase "directly and independently" is to assure that a covered loss is due exclusively to accident, and that no outside factors contributed to the final result.

Collateral Provision.   The collateral provision required to complete the full meaning of the insuring clause comprises the schedule of losses and the accompanying definitions. The usual schedule of losses follows:

Life	The principal sum
Two hands	The principal sum
Two feet	The principal sum
Sight of two eyes	The principal sum
One hand and one foot	The principal sum
One hand and sight of one eye	The principal sum
One foot and sight of one eye	The principal sum
One hand or one foot	One-half the principal sum
Sight of one eye	One-half the principal sum

Regarding hands and feet, loss is defined in the policy as dismemberment by severance at or above the wrist or ankle joints respectively. Eye loss is defined as total and irrecoverable loss of sight in that eye.

Multiple Benefits. The contract provides that no multiple benefits will be paid to a claimant on any one accident, regardless of the nature of the losses suffered. Benefit for multiple losses is limited to the largest benefit applicable to any one of the covered losses suffered. For example, a claimant who has lost both hands and the sight of one eye in a single accident would not be eligible to recover the sum of the two benefits specified in the schedule of losses. His benefit would be limited to the principal sum, which is the benefit specified for the larger of the two losses suffered.

There is no "second injury" application of the insurance. Benefits are payable only for each disability as it occurs, not for the cumulative effect of two or more disabilities. Should an insured employee lose one hand in an accident, the benefit to which he is entitled for this particular loss is one-half the principal sum, even though he may have lost the other hand in a previous accident. In the settlement of the second loss it is immaterial whether the first loss occurred before or after the effective date of the insurance.

Limitations. The limitations to the insurance afforded by the group accidental death and dismemberment cover take the form of excluded causes of loss. Viewed in the light of the insuring clause, a loss is not covered by the insurance if an excluded cause of loss is in any way a contributing factor to the loss. There are four usual exclusions, and sometimes a fifth and sixth. Usually no payment is made for a loss caused directly or indirectly, wholly or partly, by the following:

1. Disease, or bodily or mental infirmity, or medical or surgical treatment thereof.
2. Ptomaines, or bacterial infections, except infection introduced through a visible wound accidentally sustained.
3. Suicide while sane or insane, or intentionally self-inflicted injury.
4. War, or any act of war, whether declared or undeclared.

5. Injuries arising out of and in the course of any employment for wage or profit.
6. Travel or flight in any species of aircraft, except as a fare-paying passenger on a licensed passenger aircraft, provided by an incorporated passenger carrier and operated by a licensed pilot on a regularly scheduled flight between established airports.

The purpose of the first three exclusions is to do what the insuring clause may not be able to do: rule out diseases or gradual deterioration of the body and losses that are intentional or avoidable on the part of the insured. The only disease covered by the insurance is disease caused by accident, where the disease is but a link in the chain from accident to final result. The fourth exclusion in some contracts is expanded to list police action, any military service, an insurrection, or participation in a riot or felony. However, the shorter form is generally considered sufficient, because employment (and consequently the insurance) would be terminated before an employee performs any military service.

The fifth exclusion is used only when the coverage is non-occupational, and the sixth is ordinarily used only when there appears to be a noncommercial flying hazard.

Amount of Insurance. The basic benefit or amount of insurance for accidental death and dismemberment insurance is called the "principal sum." This principal sum is a flat amount of insurance in dollars, and all benefits of the insurance are in terms of this principal sum. The determination of the amount of the principal sum for which each employee is insured may be on any basis precluding individual selection by the employees.

When group accidental death and dismemberment insurance is issued in conjunction with group life insurance, the amount of the principal sum may be the same as the amount of group life insurance. Except in large cases the maximum amount of principal sum allowed is usually $20,000 or the amount of group life insurance, whichever is less. The minimum principal sum usually written is $1,000.

If the accidental death and dismemberment insurance is

issued in conjunction with an income or expense reimbursement policy, the maximum amount of principal sum may be graded according to the industrial classification of the group in question. If the insurance is written to provide nonoccupational coverage only, a single maximum limit is usually set without grading by industrial classification.

EXPENSE REIMBURSEMENT INSURANCE

Hospital Expense Insurance

Insuring Clause. A typical hospital expense insuring clause covering employees reads as follows:[3]

If any employee, while insured for Hospital Expense Insurance under this Policy, is confined as hereinafter provided in a legally constituted hospital, other than a hospital or other facility owned or operated by the United States Government or any other hospital where care is provided to the employee at federal government expense, as a result of

1. An accidental bodily injury which does not arise out of and in the course of employment, or

2. Disease for which the employee is not entitled to a benefit under any workmen's compensation law or act,

the following benefits are payable to the employee during any one continuous period of disability:

a. A Benefit in an amount equal to the charges incurred during such confinement for board and room of the employee, but not more than the amount obtained by multiplying the rate of Maximum Daily Benefit which is applicable to the employee in accordance with the provision entitled "Amounts of Insurance" contained herein, by the number of days of such confinement for which the hospital charges the employee for board and room, and in no event shall the total amount payable for all such charges exceed a sum equal to *thirty-one* times said rate of Maximum Daily Benefit: and

b. A Benefit in an amount equal to the charges which are made to the employee, in connection with such confinement,

i. by the hospital (except charges for board and room, charges arising from special nursing services, and charges for physicians' or surgeons' services), and

ii. for anesthetics and the administration thereof, and

iii. for necessary ambulance service,

---

[3] The insuring clause for dependent insurance is essentially the same.

and which are incurred before the total amount provided in subdivision (a) above for board and room of the employee becomes payable, but in no event shall the total amount payable exceed a sum equal to *ten* times said rate of Maximum Daily Benefit.

Just as in disability income insurance, the causes of loss are broadly defined as accidental bodily injuries or sickness, the only restrictions being that they be nonoccupational, that the claimant's confinement be recommended by a legally qualified physician or surgeon,[4] and that the claimant not be eligible for the services at government expense. The purpose of requiring that confinement be in a "legally constituted hospital" is to exclude payment for confinements in nursing or rest homes. The test of a loss is the result—hospital confinement, and no distinction as to cause by accident or sickness affects the claimant's eligibility for benefits. The tests applied to determine eligible hospital confinements are:

No minimum period of hospital confinement is required because of a surgical operation, or as a result of accidental bodily injury requiring emergency care, or if a board and room charge is made; otherwise, hospital confinement must be for eighteen consecutive hours or longer.

The purpose of the provision quoted above is to define the circumstances under which the hospital expense insurance applies. For emergency outpatient treatment for accidents, for surgical operations, and for expenses incurred when a claimant is charged for room and board, no minimum period of confinement is required. The purpose of requiring an eighteen-hour minimum confinement under other circumstances is to exclude from coverage outpatient treatment for sickness and diagnostic services.

Some contracts require a minimum confinement period of eighteen hours (less in some contracts), unless the confinement is for surgery or emergency treatment for accident. Under this requirement the existence of a daily room charge does not necessarily establish an eligible claim unless the

---

[4] This requirement does not appear in the insuring clause quoted, but is included under general limitations to coverage.

claimant is confined for the specified minimum period. This type of provision serves to reduce the control of the hospital over determination of an eligible claim, but many policies provide coverage if the hospital makes a room charge.

Benefits. Benefits for the daily room charge are limited to a stated amount per day, and an over-all maximum is expressed as a multiple of the daily room benefit. The multiple is the same for every member of a given group, and the most common multiples are thirty-one and seventy times the daily room benefit, although larger multiples such as 120 or 180 times are increasingly common.

Maternity benefits usually do not apply unless the pregnancy had its inception after the effective date of the insurance, but this restriction is frequently waived for female employees who become insured during the initial enrollment of a group. The restriction may be waived for dependent wives included in the initial enrollment if an extra premium is paid for the waiver. The maximum benefit for maternity is usually ten or fifteen times the daily room maximum.[5]

Separate Hospitalizations. Since there is a limit to the amount of benefits payable for any one hospital confinement, it is necessary to define in the contract what shall constitute a single hospital confinement. Until recently it was customary to provide that, for employees, two successive hospital confinements were to be considered as one confinement unless separated by a return to active employment. For dependents, two successive hospital confinements were to be considered as one confinement unless separated by a period of three months. The purpose of such requirements was to combat the possibility that an employee or dependent could secure a discharge from a hospital and then promptly re-enter a hospital, thus becoming eligible for another full period of benefits, even though the two hospital confinements were in reality one. This requirement also served to prevent an employee or

---

[5] Maximum maternity benefits may be expressed in two ways: (1) a maximum number of days of room and board care, plus an allowance for additional charges, or (2) a single maximum sum for all charges, with the maximum expressed as a multiple of the daily room rate.

dependent from receiving insurance benefits for a second confinement when two confinements were not separated as required in the policy, although two separate and distinct illnesses or accidents may have occurred. This latter result was definitely not within the purpose of the provision, since it automatically suspended the insurance from the time an employee was discharged from a hospital until his return to active work, if maximum benefits had been used. The insurance for dependents was in effect suspended for a period of three months from the time of discharge from the hospital, if maximum benefits had been used.

Such an application of the provision worked a considerable hardship upon those who suffered two separate illnesses or accidents in succession. In view of this, the major group companies have liberalized this policy provision to remove the hardship when more than one claim exists. The new and more liberal provision to cover employees states that successive periods of hospital confinement are to be considered as one period of confinement unless due to different and unrelated causes or unless separated by a return to active employment or complete recovery. Some policies require a minimum of two weeks of active work rather than just a return to active employment, and many Blue Cross plans require a separation of confinements by a period of ninety days before a new period of benefits becomes available.

Dependents' Separate Hospitalizations.   For dependents, successive periods of hospital confinement are to be considered as one period of confinement unless due to different and unrelated causes, or the second confinement follows a complete recovery. Complete recovery is usually interpreted to mean a full resumption of "usual" activities, such as a child's return to school. These provisions still aim at the original purpose of combating discharge and re-entry for what is essentially a single period of confinement, yet they do not produce a complete temporary suspension of insurance. The employee enjoys full coverage during the interval from his discharge from the hospital until his return to active work for all confinements due to causes unrelated to that of the original confinement. Similarly, dependents are fully insured following complete recovery and for all confinements due to causes unrelated to that of the original confinement, even if not fully recovered from the cause of the first confinement.[6]

Amount of Insurance. The amount of the daily room benefit for which each individual employee is insured is determined in the same manner as the amounts of insurance for the group covers already discussed. Any system is acceptable, as long as it precludes individual selection, and the most common method is to set a flat amount of daily benefit for each employee. A flat benefit for dependents is sometimes set at a lower level than the room rate for employees.

Most companies vary the maximum and minimum benefits written according to hospital rates prevailing in that locale. Daily benefits below $6.00 are uncommon today, and maximum amounts of $20 and more are offered if they appear necessary to provide the desired service to insured employees. Companies usually try to provide groups with daily benefits adequate to pay for a substantial portion of the cost of semi-private accommodations. If benefits are too high, there is a tendency to overuse insurance.

The allowance for charges other than room and board is commonly stated as a multiple of the daily room benefit. Depending upon the plan adopted by the group, the maximum allowance for additional services may be five, ten, fifteen, or twenty times the daily room benefit. The choice of the multiple of the daily benefit is for the entire group and does not vary with employees within the group. While the amount of the benefit in dollars for each employee will depend upon the daily room rate for which he is insured, each employee is insured for the same multiple of his daily room benefit. For example, in a plan providing a maximum additional services allowance of ten times the daily benefit, employees with $18 of daily room benefit will be insured up to a maximum of $180 while

---

[6] What constitutes "different and unrelated causes" is not always a clear-cut concept, but is subject to interpretation in individual cases.

employees with $20 of daily room benefit will be insured up to $200.

Most companies today offer multiples higher than twenty, and a few private carriers and most Blue Cross plans offer benefits for additional services without limit. The trend today in private carrier plans is toward offering higher multiples only on the "coinsurance" basis after charges exceed some predetermined amount. For example, a plan may provide an allowance of twenty times the daily rate plus three fourths of the next thirty times the daily room rate. This provision makes the claimant a "coinsurer" for one fourth of all the charges in excess of twenty times his daily room rate.

The benefit for extra services is available to the insured for each hospital confinement, and there is no limit to the number of times the benefits may be used within any calendar year. In most plans this allowance is available to the claimant at any time during a hospital confinement, although the clause cited at the beginning of this section limits the use of this allowance to the period for which daily room benefits are payable. The latter restriction is to prevent the claimant from using the special allowance to extend the daily benefit period by being billed for services instead of room and board. The distinction between this and the more common system is not too important except in plans with a short daily benefit period and a high maximum for special charges.

Surgical Expense

Insuring Clause. The surgical expense insuring clause usually reads as follows:

If any employee while insured for Surgical Operation Expense Insurance under this Group Policy undergoes a surgical operation specified in the Schedule of Surgical Operations and Benefits contained in this Section as a result of:

1. An accidental bodily injury which does not arise out of and in the course of employment, or

2. Disease for which the employee is not entitled to a benefit under any Workmen's Compensation Law or Act, a benefit is payable to the employee in an amount equal to the surgical fees actually charged to

the employee for the operation, but not in excess of the maximum payment specified for the operation in the applicable schedule of Surgical Operations and Benefits.

If more than one of the above described operations is performed while the employee is insured hereunder, the aforesaid benefit shall be payable for each such operation, except that the total benefit payable for all operations which are not entirely unrelated to the bodily injuries sustained in any one accident or to the same disease and which are performed before the employee either completely recovers from such injuries or disease or returns to active work and completes one day of active service, shall not exceed the Maximum Surgical Benefit applicable to the employee provided, however, that if more than one operation is performed

a. Through the same abdominal incision, the total benefit payable for all such operations shall not exceed the maximum payment specified in said schedule for that one of such operations for which the largest amount is payable; or

b. On the anus or rectum, or both (except for cancer) at any one time, the total benefit payable for all such operations shall not exceed one and one-half times the maximum payment specified in said Schedule for that one of such operations for which the largest amount is payable.

The insuring clause for surgical expense insurance defines the causes of an eligible loss as nonoccupational accidental bodily injuries or nonoccupational sickness. The important test for surgical expense insurance is the same as those applied to income reimbursement and hospital expense insurance. The result is the important thing and not close examination of the nature of the cause other than to determine that it was nonoccupational.

For both employee and dependent coverage, benefits are payable for any operation enumerated in the schedule of operations, as long as it is performed by a legally qualified physician while the individual's insurance is in force. Most contracts extend the schedule of operations by including "any cutting operation." This extension of course would not apply to operations the result of causes excluded from coverage. An obstetrical procedure is considered an insured operation, when pregnancy coverage is included.

Two or more separate operations do not usually entitle the

employee to full benefits for each unless the second and succeeding operations are from causes unrelated to the first, or the operations are separated by complete recovery or return to active work. With a schedule providing a maximum of $200, this $200 is the maximum for which an employee would be eligible for any number of operations not due to unrelated causes, unless the operations are separated by recovery or return to work.[7]

Two or more surgical procedures performed in the course of a single operation do not make the employee or dependent eligible to collect benefits for two or more separate operations. For example, it is not uncommon to remove the appendix during any operation which requires the opening of the abdominal cavity, regardless of the purpose of the operation. In such a situation the employee or dependent is eligible for the largest benefit applicable to any one of the procedures performed during the operation and not to the sum of the benefits applicable to all the procedures. As stated in the insuring clause quoted, a higher maximum may be allowed for certain multiple procedures.

Amount of Insurance. The amount of surgical expense insurance is expressed in a schedule of relative values which provides for reimbursement of the employee or dependent up to a maximum amount specified for particular operations. The maximum amounts payable according to the schedule are not intended to represent what the surgeon's charge should be, but are the maximum amounts for which the employee will be paid for the specified surgical operations. There are several schedules in use, but the most widely used schedule today provides for a maximum benefit of $200 for any operation, and the amounts allowed for all operations are in about the same ratio to current charges for such operations. Depending upon the plan selected by the group, multiples of these standard schedules may be written to provide any desired maximum up to $300, $400, or more.

---

[7] The eligibility tests for claims under surgical expense insurance are the same as those discussed above under hospital expense insurance.

Benefits for obstetrical procedures usually are not provided for pregnancies existing on the effective date of the individual employee's or dependent's insurance. However, plans are written providing immediate obstetrical benefits for female employees, if these employees become insured within thirty-one days after the effective date of the master contract. Immediate obstetrical benefits for dependents are usually provided only if they are insured during initial enrollment and if an extra initial premium is paid.

Basic Medical Expense

The nature of the benefits provided and the amount of benefits depend upon the particular plan of medical expense insurance issued to cover a group. These plans are not uniform in all particulars among different insurance companies, but they provide generally the same coverage, which consists of benefits for physician's visits, diagnostic procedures outside a hospital, or both. In the following discussion the different plans available are grouped according to the nature of the benefits provided.

In-hospital Plan. The in-hospital plan provides for reimbursement for expenses incurred for visits by a physician to the employee or dependent while the employee or dependent is confined to a legally constituted and operated hospital as an admitted inpatient upon the recommendation of a legally qualified physician. This plan provides no benefits for visits at the home of the insured, at the physician's office, or to a surgeon following a surgical operation.

There is no maximum applied to the reimbursement per visit nor to the number of visits per day for which the insured may be paid. The maximum amount of reimbursement the employee or dependent is entitled to receive for all visits is an aggregate amount which accumulates at a fixed rate for each day of hospital confinement. Depending upon the plan adopted by the group, this rate may be either $3.00 or $4.00 per day of hospital confinement, but the aggregate amount is limited to a maximum such as $150 for a $3.00 plan and $200 for a

$4.00 plan. The selection of the accumulation rate is made for the group as a whole, and the members of the group are not allowed to select this rate individually.

Total Disability Plan. A total disability plan of medical expense insurance is written to cover employees only, since it would be practically impossible to determine when total disability exists for the majority of dependents, who are not gainfully employed.

Benefits under this plan of insurance cover visits by a physician whether the employee is in or out of a hospital. For charges for physicians' visits to the employee while confined to a hospital, reimbursement to the employee may be provided on the same basis as the in-hospital plan. Each day of hospital confinement (up to a maximum number of days) adds a stated number of dollars to the maximum amounts for which the employee may be reimbursed for these in-hospital visits.

For visits outside a hospital, the benefits are placed on an amount-per-visit basis.[8] Depending upon the plan adopted by the group, reimbursement is provided for physician's charges for not more than any one visit on any one day, up to a maximum of: (1) $2.00 for each visit at a physician's office and $3.00 for each visit at the employee's home, or (2) $4.00 for each office visit and $6.00 for each home visit. A few plans provide no limit to the number of visits for which the employee may be reimbursed during the period of disability, but most plans provide a maximum amount, such as $150.

The deductible principle is applied to plans providing reimbursement on an amount-per-visit basis, and the policyholder may elect that one of the following bases be used:

1. No benefits are payable for the first two visits, whether disability is due to accident or sickness.

2. Benefits are payable beginning with the first visit when disability

---

[8] When the total disability plan is written in connection with income reimbursement insurance, in-hospital visits may be reimbursed on an amount-per-visit basis, but the total disability plan usually provides benefits for in-hospital visits on the in-hospital basis when written in connection with hospital expense insurance.

is due to accident, but no benefits will be paid for the first two (or three) visits when disability is due to sickness.

3. Benefits begin at the end of the income reimbursement waiting period.

These exclusions are not applied to visits made while the employee is confined to a hospital, but hospital visits made while the employee is not confined as an admitted inpatient are reimbursed on the same basis as office visits and are subject to any exclusion for initial visits which may apply.

Since no deductible is applied to benefits for hospital visits, no deductible is applied to out-of-hospital visits when these visits represent a continuation of a claim for which in-hospital benefits are payable. This practice is in recognition of the fact that it would be an improper application of the deductible principle to treat a loss continuation as a new loss.

Nondisability Plan. As its name implies, the nondisability plan does not require disability before insurance benefits are available. The benefits provided are usually the same as those provided by the total disability plan, for both in-hospital and out-of-hospital visits. Under some plans, benefits are payable beginning with the physician's first visit, whether the claimant is in or out of the hospital, and total disability is not required to make the insured eligible for benefits. The fact that the charge for a physician's visit has been incurred is sufficient to establish a claim.

Other nondisability plans provide essentially the same protection with similar maximum benefits, but with a waiting period applied to the first few visits. For accidents, benefits may begin with the first, second, third, or fourth call, but for sickness, benefits seldom begin prior to the third call. Since total disability is not required, control on the waiting period requirement is achieved by defining a new series of calls as beginning when two sickness calls are separated by more than twenty days.

The usual occupational and pregnancy exclusions apply, and calls are not covered when made by the operating surgeon after the operation is performed. Usually contracts exclude benefits for eye examinations, X-ray examinations, laboratory examinations, and periodic physical examinations.

Since total disability is not required, the nondisability form of medical expense insurance may be issued to cover dependents as well as employees. This is broader and more expensive coverage than the total disability plans provide. Its main advantage is that it covers costs which may be incurred in order to *prevent* total disability.

X-ray and Laboratory Examination Plan. Another plan of medical expense insurance provides for reimbursement of the employee or dependent for charges on diagnostic X-ray or most laboratory examinations, but excludes urinalysis and X-ray therapy. It is customarily written in conjunction with hospital and surgical expense insurance, and it provides no benefits for X-ray and laboratory examinations performed while the employee or dependent is confined to a hospital. When these charges are incurred during a hospital confinement, they are covered under hospital expense insurance. Some contracts do not exclude in-hospital benefits completely, but exclude them only if the same benefits are payable under hospital expense insurance.

An employee or dependent is entitled to reimbursement for the actual charges incurred for X-ray or laboratory examination up to a maximum amount set forth in the contract. The maximum may be a flat sum or a schedule of benefits for specified examinations. Whichever system is used, an over-all maximum is applied for all examinations. Most contracts provide that the maximum reimbursement during any twelve-month period will be $25, but some provide a maximum reimbursement of $50 or $75. Other plans provide a maximum of $25 or $50 for all examinations due to any one accident or disease without a specific restriction on the maximum reimbursement during any benefit year.

Insuring Clauses. There is no common or single insuring clause for use in medical expense insurance, because many different plans of insurance are written, and the insuring clause must be designed to provide the benefits of the particular plan of insurance offered. The insuring clause is not complete without an accompanying definition of an insured loss, and this definition varies with the type of medical expense plan selected by a group. Most medical expense plans cover charges incurred for visits for treatment by a physician, or for X-ray or laboratory examinations, or a given plan may cover both. That part of the insuring clause which states the covered causes of loss is uniform even between different plans of benefit. Under a plan providing insurance benefits for visits for treatment by a physician, the causes of loss are the same for all plans and may be expressed as follows:

Upon receipt of due proof that any employee, while insured for Medical Expense Benefits, shall have incurred expenses for visits for treatment of the employee by a physician legally licensed to practice medicine and surgery, and that such treatment is on account of nonoccupational accidental bodily injuries or nonoccupational sickness, the company will pay . . .[9]

For a plan providing insurance for X-ray or laboratory examinations, the causes of loss are defined in much the same way:

Upon receipt of due proof that any employee, while insured for Medical Expense Benefits, shall have incurred expenses for X-ray or laboratory examinations of the employee (other than urinalyses and excluding X-ray therapy) made or recommended by a physician legally licensed to practice medicine and surgery and in connection with the diagnosis of nonoccupational accidental bodily injuries or nonoccupational sickness, the company will pay . . .

The causes of an eligible loss are nonoccupational accidental bodily injuries and nonoccupational sickness. The result insured against in the first clause cited is a visit (or visits) for treatment by a licensed physician. In the second clause cited the results insured against are expenses incurred for diagnostic X-ray or laboratory examinations (excluding urinalysis) made in connection with the diagnosis of nonoccupational accidental bodily injuries or nonoccupational sickness.

---

[9] For dependent coverage the clause is practically the same, with the words "dependent" or "wife and child" substituted for "employee."

Limitations Applicable to Medical Expense Insurance.
The only limitation that excludes a cause of loss to an employee
under most medical expense insurance plans, other than the
requirement that it must be nonoccupational, is the exclusion
of medical visits in connection with pregnancy or resulting
childbirth, abortion, or miscarriage. Pregnancy is also specifically excluded as a cause of loss in dependents' coverage, as is
accidental bodily injury arising out of and in the course of employment, and some contracts provide that no reimbursement
will be made for expenses incurred for treatment or examination of a dependent in a mental hospital or hospital for mental
defectives.

All other limitations are exclusions based on the nature of
the charge incurred. Contracts usually provide that no payment will be made for expenses incurred for (1) dental work
or treatments, dental X-ray, or eye refractions, (2) visits by
the surgeon after an operation for which benefits are payable
under the surgical benefits provisions of the group policy, or
(3) X-ray or laboratory examinations performed while the
insured is confined in a hospital. As in all forms of health insurance for dependents, dependents are not eligible for benefits as dependents if they are eligible for benefits as employees
or former employees of the employer.

Major Medical Expense

The most recent addition to the group health field is the
major medical or catastrophe loss cover. Basic hospital, surgical,
and medical expense insurance are limited by the cost factor
as to total benefits for a single loss. Major medical attempts to
extend coverage far beyond that of basic by excluding from
coverage at least some of the smaller but more frequent losses
and establishing maximum benefit limits such as $10,000 or as
much as $20,000.

Early forms of major medical were designed to supplement
a base plan of hospital, surgical, and medical expense insurance or to provide coverage for those of such economic status
that a base plan was unnecessary. The more recently developed

comprehensive approach generally sets deductible amounts low enough so that an additional plan of basic coverage is not necessary. This approach makes it possible to provide coverage for medical expenditures falling within the coverage range of either the regular basic or the early major medical types of plans. Premium costs for this comprehensive form of insurance are kept to a marketable level by the application of a deductible at the beginning of the medical expense range to rule out coverage of normal, expected, or budgetable medical expenses.

Scope of Major Medical. Major medical is broad in coverage in that it includes practically all types of necessary medical expenses, whether the insured individual is in the hospital or not, and there are few limitations as to types of expenditures covered. Present contracts generally set forth the types or categories of expenses covered, and coverage without restriction as to amount for each is usually provided for the following:

1. Doctors' charges for diagnosis, treatment, or surgery.
2. Charges for services of a registered nurse.
3. Drugs and medicines requiring a prescription.
4. Anesthesia and its administration.
5. Diagnostic procedures and transfusions.
6. Oxygen.
7. Rental of therapeutic equipment.
8. Charges by a radiologist or physiotherapist.
9. Hospital charges for room, board, and routine services including general nursing care. Semiprivate accommodations may be covered in full, but a maximum daily room and board allowance is usually specified if the claimant chooses private accommodations.

Most plans provide that the insurer is liable for payment when expenses have been incurred, and this of course leads to coverage for pre-existing conditions. With large amounts of benefit involved, this presents a more serious underwriting problem than coverage of such conditions presents in basic covers.[10] Most plans today provide some restrictions on cover-

---

[10] See discussion by A. M. Wilson, *Group Proceedings of the Health and Accident Underwriters Conference,* 1952, pp. 64–66.

age for pre-existing conditions. Many plans exclude coverage for pre-existing conditions unless the claimant completes after the effective date of his insurance a period of ninety consecutive days free of medical expense for the pre-existing condition. Some plans apply the ninety-day restriction, but permit coverage for the pre-existing condition after one year of insurance coverage in the plan or the completion of six months of active employment.

Major medical plans usually do not require that total disability exist before benefits are payable, because this would seriously limit the value of the coverage. Substantial medical expenses can be incurred without the existence of disability in the usual sense; in fact, substantial expenses may be incurred in order that insured individuals can continue to work. However, some contracts do require at least a temporary period of total disability to start the operation of the major medical benefit formula. Most contracts do provide an extended insurance benefit which requires continuous total disability from the time the insurance is terminated. This extended benefit provides continued protection, for three months or as long as a year in some plans, on claims in progress when insurance is terminated for any cause except nonpayment of premiums.

Although major medical is extremely broad in coverage, not all types of medical expenditures are covered. Most contracts include two groups of exclusions: those excluding certain causes of loss and those excluding certain types of expenses. Under excluded causes, payment is usually excluded for expenses due to:

1. Accidental bodily injuries arising out of or in the course of employment.
2. Disease for which the claimant is entitled to workmen's compensation benefits.
3. Pregnancy, except when surgical procedures are required or there are complications of pregnancy for the mother or child.
4. Alcoholism or narcotic habits.
5. War.
6. Intentionally self-inflicted injury.

As to types of expenses excluded, contracts usually provide that no payment will be made for expenses incurred for:

1. Dental treatment or cosmetic surgery, unless caused by a non-occupational accident while the claimant is insured.
2. Health examinations, normal eye and ear examinations, and fitting of glasses and hearing aids.
3. Services that are not certified as necessary by a licensed doctor of medicine.
4. Medical services for which the claimant is not required to make payment.
5. Medical services rendered by a facility of the federal government or a state government.
6. Services or supplies that are unreasonably priced or not reasonably necessary in light of the disease or injury being treated.

Both groups of exclusions concern medical expenses that are considered to be either uninsurable or likely to be insured in other ways, if insurance is necessary at all. Many plans include also a nonduplication provision which removes coverage for expenses reimbursed by another group plan under which the employee or a member of his family might be eligible.

Deductible Provisions.   Major medical plans use the deductible provision in order to (1) eliminate the administrative expense of small claims, (2) reduce total claim cost by elimination of small claims and sometimes a portion of large claims, and (3) discourage unnecessary use of insurance.

Two general types of deductibles are used, depending upon the place in medical expenses that the deductible is imposed. The "initial" deductible is applied at the beginning of medical expenses, and the insured person must bear the deductible amount of expenses before major medical benefits become available. This type of deductible is used in major medical plans designed for those who do not need coverage under basic plans, and a scale of deductibles based on salary classes is sometimes used, so "major" losses will be defined relative to income. Under such a plan, deductibles may be set as high as $1,000 or more.

The "initial" deductible is also used in the comprehensive major medical plans designed to replace basic medical expense covers. Such plans may provide a very small deductible, such as $25, and many plans do not apply the deductible at all to hospital expenses.

The "corridor" deductible is applied somewhere in the middle of medical expenses after benefits from basic covers are exhausted. The purpose of the corridor differs from that of the initial deductible: it is not designed to exclude payments for small losses but to make the claimant a "coinsurer" for the first $100 or more after basic benefits have been used. Many plans, however, make the corridor type of deductible apply as an initial deductible as to expenses not covered at all by the base plan. In plans of this type the deductible amount can be satisfied by any combination of medical expenses not covered by the base plan, provided they are defined as "eligible" expenses under the major medical contract. Such a combination might include amounts by which a daily room charge exceeds the base plan benefit, and such items as physicians' charges for home calls, which may not be covered by the base plan.

A mixture of the corridor and initial deductibles was used in some early major medical plans. This type provided that the deductible was to be the greater of a given number of dollars or base plan benefits. When base plan benefits proved to be below the stated number of dollars, the deductible was a corridor of an unpredictable amount. When base plan benefits exceeded the stated number of dollars, the deductible was initial, so that basic and major medical did not overlap.

Methods of Applying Deductibles. Regardless of the type of deductible used, the major medical contract must define the method by which the deductible is to be applied before benefits become available. There are in general use four methods of determining which covered medical expenses are applicable in satisfying the deductible.

1. Some major medical plans apply the deductible to each insured person for each separate illness or accident, and

medical expenses incurred for a different and unrelated cause are treated under a separate deductible application. Since expenditures for chronic illnesses may be substantial over a lifetime but not "major" in a relatively short time, most plans provide a "benefit period" restriction of some type with respect to the application of the deductible. Some plans require a minimum expenditure such as $50 during a period of ninety days; otherwise a new benefit period is established and the deductible must be applied again. Some plans provide that a benefit period terminates six months after a claimant returns to active work, and for subsequent expenditures the deductible would be applied again.

Since the per-cause method of deductible application could result in requiring the insured to bear more than one deductible in a short period of time, the method results in lower premium cost than is possible with some other forms of deductible. From a coverage standpoint, however, this method of deductible application leaves unanswered the problem faced by families who suffer more than one major illness in a short time. The problem has been only partially solved by modifying the plan to apply the deductible only once per family in a "common disaster" or accident injuring more than one family member. The method also creates many problems in claims administration for the insurer, because it is frequently difficult to determine if a particular medical expenditure is "related" to the cause for which claim has previously been made.

2. A second method of deductible application assesses the deductible amount against each individual in an insured family during a "benefit year." Under this method the benefit year begins when the individual first incurs a covered medical expense and terminates at the end of twelve months or earlier if the claimant is free from medical expense for some period stated in the contract. This method permits each person to receive credit against his deductible for all his covered expenditures for medical care regardless of the cause of the expense, and the insurance begins to pay when expenditures during the benefit period exceed the deductible amount.

The second method solves one of the problems inherent in the per-cause method, in that an individual will not suffer two applications of the deductible in a short time just because he has two different diseases or accidents. Neither of these two, however, solve the problem for the family when two or more family members suffer major illnesses in a short time. However, the benefit-year method usually applies the "common disaster" provision found in the per-cause method. The obvious objections to the benefit-period method of deductible application are the necessity of detailed record keeping by the family and the burdensome detail of determining eligibility for insurance benefits.

3. A modification of the benefit-year method involves the application of the deductible once to each individual in each calendar year, but with the "common disaster" provision found in the two methods just discussed. The use of calendar rather than benefit year overcomes a large part of the problem of determining eligibility for benefits, although the method has all the other disadvantages of the benefit period method. An arbitrary cut-off date at the end of each calendar year makes possible a double application of a deductible to an individual claimant within a short time, although most plans provide for at least a three-month separation of deductibles. This separation is effected by a carry-over system, which permits the individual to apply toward the deductible in a given calendar year those expenditures which were incurred and applied to a deductible in the last three months of the previous year. Under this method a person who had entirely met his deductible by expenditures during the last three months in any year would have no deductible in the following calendar year.

4. A family budget method of deductible application makes major medical benefits available for all covered medical expenditures of an entire family as soon as family medical expenditures exceed the monthly or annual deductible amount. The amount of the deductible may vary from $25 to $250 a month, depending on employee salary, and many plans waive

the deductible in any month in which total expenditures exceed a specified amount.

This is probably the simplest method of deductible application for the insured person to understand, although claim filing and administration tend to be burdensome to the insured and the insurer. The method does provide excellent coverage, since it holds the area of self-assumption of medical expense by the insured to a predetermined budgetable amount during each calender month or year.

Coinsurance Provision. Major medical contracts require the claimant to bear some portion of his own medical expenditures in excess of the deductible amount. This portion may be 15, 20, or 25 per cent, depending upon the particular major medical plan. There are two purposes of paying less than all the medical expenses in excess of the deductible. First, the requirement that the claimant pay perhaps one fifth or one fourth of the charges over the deductible should discourage the claimant from using unnecessary medical services, such as "luxury" hospital accommodations. The second purpose of coinsurance is to give the claimant a direct financial interest in the amounts he is charged for services rendered to him. However, the use of coinsurance has not been entirely successful, because payment of only 75 or 80 per cent of medical expenses in excess of the deductible amount will not have the same relative effect on all claimants receiving the same services. Experience has shown clearly that persons in higher income groups demand and are willing to pay part of the costs of the best care available.

Maximum Benefit Provisions. All major medical plans use some method of limiting the benefits available under the plan, because completely "open" contracts could produce claims not anticipated in premium rates charged. Maximum limits are usually expressed either as a lifetime maximum for each individual or as a maximum for each individual during a calendar or benefit year. Some plans provide both a lifetime maximum and a calendar or benefit year maximum, with the latter set at perhaps one half the lifetime maximum.

Maximum lifetime benefits may be applied to each individual for all covered expenditures regardless of cause, or the maximum may be applied to each separate accident or illness. When the maximum is applied to each separate accident or sickness, the aggregate amount which the individual might collect is limited only by the number of different accidents or illnesses that the claimant might suffer. If the maximum amount and other plan provisions are equal, the per-cause maximum would be better coverage than the lifetime maximum for all causes. However, most plans which provide a lifetime maximum benefit for all causes will permit reinstatement of amounts used, provided the claimant has used at least $1,000 of benefit and can provide satisfactory evidence of insurability to the insurer.

Types of Major Medical Plans. As indicated in the discussions above, there are many ways in which major medical plans can express statements of covered medical expenses, deductible applications, coinsurance, and maximum benefit limitations. It is therefore virtually impossible to classify and "label" major medical contracts as to specific "types" because of the many forms such plans may take. However, each plan must state (1) its scope of coverage, (2) the exclusions of causes and expenses from coverage, (3) the type of deductible, (4) the method of satisfying the deductible, (5) the coinsurance percentage, and (6) the limitations on maximum benefit. Perhaps with the passage of time such plans will fall into specific patterns which can be readily indentified.

Polio and Dread Disease Covers

The offer of special insurance benefits for poliomyelitis and other so-called "dread disease" causes of loss was due primarily to policyholder demands for protection. Many in the group insurance field recognize that this approach to coverage of the disability hazard is completely wrong. Development of effective poliomyelitis vaccine and continued growth of major medical insurance will doubtless reduce both the need for and the popular appeal of this type of coverage.

There is no question that financial losses to the individual can be serious when the causes of loss are such diseases as poliomyelitis, leukemia, tularemia, meningitis, encephalitis, tetanus, typhoid, and smallpox. The relatively low frequency of these diseases is not proof that they should not be insured as causes of loss. It should be possible to offer worthwhile insurance protection against these diseases at reasonable cost, if the cover can be tied to other forms of group insurance to keep the expense rate low.

These covers are sometimes written on a blanket reimbursement basis, with benefits limited to a maximum amount of $1,000, $5,000, or $10,000 for medical care because of a covered disease. Insurers have found that there is little or no underwriting control when insurance is written on this basis, because there is no limit (other than the over-all maximum) to the amount that can be claimed for any one type of medical service, such as charges for diagnosis. Most insurers have attempted to remedy this situation by providing scheduled maximum amounts of reimbursement for specific services, with an over-all maximum applied to some and a daily maximum applied to others. The problem stems from the fact that charges for medical services of almost all types are based largely on the individual's ability to pay, and the "inside" limits at least restrict the amounts by which the insurance contributes to the claimant's ability to pay.

Blue Cross and Blue Shield plans which include the dread disease type of coverage often do not apply scheduled maximum amounts for specific services. The relationship of these plans to the hospitals and doctors providing services gives these plans some advantage in controlling charges made to patients.

CHAPTER III

PRINCIPAL CONTRACT PROVISIONS

THE master contract provisions discussed in the preceding chapter apply to specific health insurance covers, but many provisions must appear in the contract regardless of the group coverage provided. In some contracts these provisions are repeated for each cover; that is, each cover has a complete "policy" which could stand alone. However, the trend is toward simplifying the group contract by eliminating repetition. Since these provisions need appear only once regardless of the number and combination of covers, they are grouped as general provisions in the master contract. Some provisions discussed below concerning rights and duties of certificate holders are not the same for all covers, and the variations are brought out in the following discussion.

The 1940 Commissioners' Model Bill pertaining to group health insurance contained fifteen standard provisions, but this bill has not been adopted in any state. However, the Uniform Standard Provisions Law, prepared by the Health and Accident Underwriters Conference in 1950, has been followed substantially in thirty states. Since practices are uniform in jurisdictions with and without standard provision legislation, no distinction will be made in the following discussion between provisions that are merely usual and those that are standard by law in some states. The remaining master contract provisions are grouped under three headings:

1. The rights and duties of the policyholder.
2. The rights and duties of the certificate holder.
3. Miscellaneous contract provisions.

RIGHTS AND DUTIES OF THE POLICYHOLDER

Effective Date and Consideration

The effective date of the policy is usually agreed upon when the preliminary application is submitted but is subject to acceptance of the group by the home office, the payment of the initial premium, and meeting the minimum participation requirements for the group. The policy is issued in consideration of the insurance application and the initial premium payment, which is determined by applying the applicable premium rates to the total amounts of benefits in force. Payment of any premium after the first is a condition precedent to continuance of the insurance, subject to the termination provisions of the contract.

Termination of the Master Contract

The policies of the major group carriers specify that termination of the master contract is automatic for a default in premium payment, and that cancellation may be effected by the insurer on any policy anniversary or subsequent premium due date if the minimum group requirements are not met.

Cancellation on Policy Anniversary. Some contracts provide that the insurer may terminate the contract on any policy anniversary by giving written notice to the employer at least thirty days prior to the anniversary. The employer has the same right of termination.

Cancellation for Failure to Meet Minimum Requirements. The insurer reserves the right to terminate the contract on any premium due date after the first policy anniversary if the minimum group requirements are not met. Depending upon state laws and company underwriting rules, the minimum number of employees required may be as many as twenty-five or as few as two. Requiring a minimum number is only half the story, since that alone would not be enough to combat selection against the insurer by individual employees. Just as the insurer cannot permit complete freedom of choice in joining a group, neither can it allow complete freedom of choice in withdrawing from a group. Control of this factor is secured by requiring the participation of a minimum percentage of eligible employees. Employees become insured and remain insured automatically when eligible if the group is noncontributory, so that 100 per cent participation is effected without any employee action. When the employee contributes to premium payments and consequently is given a choice concerning coverage retention, it is necessary in practice and by legal definition in some states to require that some minimum percentage of the eligible employees remain insured. The minimum usually required is 75 per cent.

Employer's Reports to the Insurance Company

The master contract requires that the employer report to the insurer certain information necessary to service the group plan. The following information is required from all except the self-accounting groups: the names of all employees as they become insured; the ages, amounts of insurance, and effective dates of insurance on newly insured employees and all changes in status and terminations in the group. Changes in status and termination are to be reported within one month after they occur, and the insurer reserves the right to examine the pertinent records of the employer at any reasonable time to verify any statement furnished the insurer pursuant to the policy provisions.

The contracts usually provide that employees qualified for the insurance under a master contract are not deprived of their insurance by the employer's failure to report them to the insurer. This applies to both contributory and noncontributory groups; an employee in a noncontributory group is qualified when he has met the eligibility requirements, and an employee in a contributory group is qualified when he has met the eligibility requirements and has made the required election for the insurance. Similarly, the termination of an employee's insurance is determined solely by the "Individual Terminations" provisions of the contract, and the employer's failure to report the termination of the insurance of any employee does not effect a continuation of the insurance.

Payment of Premiums

Any premium after the first is payable by the employer at the home office of the insurer or to an authorized representative of the insurer on or before the due date. Premiums under most group policies are payable monthly, but they may be paid quarterly, semiannually, or annually, if arrangements are made in advance with the insurance company.

Adjustment of Premiums

Adjustments in the amount of monthly premium payable due to changes in the amounts of insurance are made on the next monthly premium due date after the changes in the amounts of insurance have occurred. There is usually no premium adjustment for partial months, either debit or credit. This procedure for handling partial months of different amounts of insurance simplifies premium accounting considerably, even if the increases and decreases in insurance do not exactly balance out. However, provision is made that any monthly premium will include any adjustment in past premiums required by changes in amounts of insurance which should have appeared on earlier premium statements. Premium payments for any individual employee continue while the employee is drawing benefits under the insurance, if the employee remains insured under the policy.

Premium adjustments are made at the end of each policy year on policies with premiums paid quarterly, semiannually, or annually, although some companies make monthly billing adjustments. Final adjustment is based on some average of benefits in force during the year, if adjustments are not made monthly.

Dividend or Retroactive Rate Reduction

The contracts contain a provision concerning retroactive cost adjustments in the form of annual dividends on participating policies or premium refunds on nonparticipating policies. The participating policies usually state that dividends, if any, to be dstributed upon the policy will be ascertained and distributed annually by the insurance company as each policy anniversary occurs. However, some contracts provide that the group is not eligible for a dividend unless its policy has been continued in force by payment of all premiums up to the policy anniversary upon which the dividend is to be distributed. The dividend to be distributed under a policy will be paid in cash to the policyholder, unless written notice has been given by the policyholder to the insurance company that the dividend is to be applied to the payment of premiums on the policy.

Nonparticipating policies provide that, if experience of a group is favorable, a rate reduction may be made retroactive for one year. Any retroactive rate reduction will result in a refund of the amount by which the premium is reduced. Dividends under participating policies usually are not contingent upon policy renewal, but retroactive adjustments under some nonparticipating policies are contingent upon renewal.

Grace Period

A grace period of thirty-one days is granted to the employer for the payment of every premium after the first, and the master contract continues in force during this period. The procedure in health insurance is the same as that in group life insurance, where the policy continues in force during the grace period unless notice of termination has been given; and the policyholder is liable to the insurance company for the payment of a pro rata premium for the time the policy was in force during the grace period.

However, some contracts provide that the master contract is terminated on the due date of any premium not paid before the end of the grace period. No prorating is attempted, and no losses during the grace period are covered unless the premium is paid before the expiration of the grace period.

Assignment of the Master Contract

The master contracts in use by some group companies provide "that no assignment of this policy by the employer will be binding upon the company unless in writing and until filed at its home office." The contracts also provide that "the insurance company assumes no responsibility for the validity of any assignment." Since the employer (policyholder) is prohibited by law from benefiting from the insurance, the only assignable "interest" available to the employer would be whatever value may exist in retaining the group insurance as originally written. This value may of course be considerable when a change of ownership of the business occurs, if the group has built up a retroactive rate reduction credit.

RIGHTS AND DUTIES OF CERTIFICATE HOLDERS

Nature of the Certificate

The certificates issued to members of groups insured by group health policies are held as evidence of insurance only in most jurisdictions and not contracts between any of the parties. The certificate usually carries a statement to this effect on the first page, with the additional statement that the insurance described in the certificate is effective only if the employee is eligible for insurance and becomes and remains insured under the particular master contract terms, provisions, and conditions.

The master contract states that the insurer will issue to the employer (or other policyholder), for delivery to each employee insured under the policy, an individual certificate setting forth a statement on the insurance protection to which each employee is entitled under the policy and to whom the benefits are payable. The master contract also states that the policy and the application of the policyholder, together with the individual applications, if any, of the employees insured, shall constitute the entire contract between the parties.

Since the certificate is generally held not to be a part of the contract of insurance, its principal value is of a practical rather than a legal nature. It serves as tangible evidence of the insurance to the employee, which may be of importance to his sense of individual security. Probably the greatest practical value of the certificate lies in the fact that it presents a summary of the insurance protection afforded by the master contract; the employee has printed descriptions of his insurance, kept up to date either by endorsement or issuance of a new certificate when changes in the insurance occur.

An employee may receive only one certificate, or he may receive a certificate for each of the insurance covers provided by group health insurance. Usually no more than three certificates are used to provide group life and all the health covers. The current tendency is to use one certificate with appropriate endorsements or inserts for all covers.

Effective Date of Individual Insurance

The certificate usually states specifically the effective date of the individual employee's insurance, but may only state that the certificate holder is eligible for the described benefits if he "becomes and remains insured under the master contract in accordance with its provisions, terms, and conditions."

Noncontributory Groups. No positive action is required of the employee if he makes no contribution to premium payments, and the insurance of the employee (for himself and his dependents, if applicable) becomes effective on the eligibility date or the effective date of the master contract, whichever is later. However, whether a plan is contributory or noncontributory, an employee not actively at work usually cannot become insured until his return to active work, and dependents who are confined in a hospital cannot become insured for hospital or surgical expense benefits until confinement is terminated. However, the active work restriction is sometimes waived under negotiated plans where individual eligibility is based on work history.

Contributory Groups. When the employee pays a part of the premiums, the insurance does not become effective until the employee has elected the insurance. If this election is made on or before the eligibility date, then the effective date of insurance is the eligibility date; but the date of the election of the insurance, or the next payroll deduction date, becomes the effective date when the election is made after the eligibility date and within thirty-one days thereafter. The employee may elect the insurance at any time; but when the election is delayed longer than thirty-one days after the eligibility date, the chances of selection against the insurer are greatly increased. Accordingly, a common practice is to require that the employee and dependents produce satisfactory evidence of insurability if election was delayed, or if previously terminated insurance is being reinstated. In lieu of evidence of insurability of a dependent, benefits may be deferred. If the employee is already insured with respect to other dependents, newly acquired dependents are usually included automatically, subject to any required adjustment in premiums and the employee's contributions. The master contract and the certificate include a definition of dependents. The usual definition limits coverage of dependents to wife (sometimes husband) and dependent children within a given age range, which may be from birth to age nineteen or even older if the child is in school or college. Children can, therefore, be covered soon after birth and can remain covered until such age as they may be expected to become independent of the family unit.

Termination of Individual Insurance

Master contracts and certificates provide that the insurance of an employee or dependent terminates automatically if the master contract is terminated, upon the cessation of premium payments for the employee's or dependent's insurance, or if the employee fails to pay any required contribution. These provisions apply to each of the group health covers, and are in addition to the provisions for termination of specific covers discussed below.

Income Reimbursement Insurance. The income reimbursement insurance of an individual employee is terminated automatically upon the termination of his employment in the classes of employees eligible for insurance under the policy. Termination of employment is further defined to apply to employees who are retired, pensioned, granted leave of absence, or temporarily laid off.[1] An employee may have his insurance terminated automatically, even though he continues to work for the same employer, if he is changed to a class of employees not eligible under the group insurance plan. Cessation of active work is considered a termination of employment; but if an employee is disabled, he is considered employed during any period for which he is drawing benefits under the policy. The insurance is continued throughout this period the employee is receiving benefits, but only if the employer continues to pay premiums for the disabled employee. If the employee fails to return to active work at or by the end of the period for which he drew benefits, then the insurance terminates automatically and premium payments on account of his insurance are discontinued. Later return to work requires reinstatement before the insurance becomes effective again.

The accidental death and dismemberment insurance of an individual employee is terminated automatically upon the termination of his employment in the classes of eligible employees. Cessation of active work constitutes a termination of employment, except that under certain circumstances the employer may report the employee as still employed by filing written notice and continuing the payment of premiums for the employee's insurance. When the employee becomes disabled by injury or disease, he may be regarded as still employed for the full period of disability. The employee may remain insured for the full period of disability, since there is no "benefit period" for accidental death and dismemberment insurance as there is for income reimbursement coverage. Similarly, the employee may be regarded as still employed

---

[1] Under some contracts the employer may elect to continue the insurance for employees temporarily laid off or on leaves of absence. However, a definite time limit is usually prescribed, and the employer is required to treat all such employees in a uniform manner to prevent adverse selection.

up to a specified maximum period (seldom more than three months) for a leave of absence or layoff. Unless the employee returns to active work at the expiration of the period for which his insurance is continued, the insurance automatically terminates.

Expense Reimbursement Insurance. The master contract provisions concerning the termination of an individual employee's hospital, surgical, medical, and major medical expense insurance establish almost exactly the same rules as those applied to income reimbursement insurance, except that hospital and surgical expense insurance are not terminated because maximum benefits have been received. Benefits under these two covers would be payable for a claim if the cause is not related to the cause of the claim for which maximum benefits have already been paid. However, some Blue Cross plans require a separation of hospital confinements by a period of ninety days before a new maximum period of benefits becomes available. Some contracts provide that a disabled employee may be considered still employed for the continuation of his hospital and surgical expense insurance up to a maximum of three months. Most major medical expense contracts permit reinstatement of insurance after $1,000 of benefits have been paid, if the employee can show satisfactory evidence of insurability.

The termination of an employee's expense reimbursement insurance is based on his employment, and termination of a dependent's insurance is also based on the employee's employment. The dependent's relationship to the group is through the employee. The expense reimbursement lines of insurance are not written to cover dependents but to insure the employee on behalf of his dependents when he is covered by the same insurance. The contract provides also that termination of the employee's insurance automatically brings termination of the dependent's insurance. A dependent's insurance is terminated if the dependent becomes eligible for the same insurance as an employee.

In addition to automatic termination of insurance for dependents at termination of the employee's insurance, the termination of expense reimbursement insurance of a dependent may be based on the dependency status. Contracts provide that a dependent wife's insurance ends automatically if her marriage to the employee is terminated by divorce or legal separation. For a dependent child the insurance terminates automatically when the child reaches a certain age or marries. The date of the termination of the dependent child's insurance is the premium due date falling on or following the date of the marriage or the date on which the maximum age was attained.

Extended Insurance Benefits

Master contracts provide that if an employee's or dependent's hospital, surgical, or basic medical expense insurance is terminated for any cause, the employee or dependent is entitled to a three-month period of extended benefit eligibility if he was disabled at the time his insurance ceased and remains disabled. Major medical generally provides from three months to a year of extended benefits under the same circumstances. Total disability is required and is defined in some contracts as existing when the claimant is "continuously prevented from engaging in any occupation for compensation or profit." To be eligible for hospital expense benefits, the claimant must have been confined to a hospital while disabled within three months from the termination of his insurance, and for the cause of his disability at the time his insurance was terminated. The claimant is eligible for surgical benefits if the operation is performed within three months after the termination of the insurance and while the disability continues. Most medical expense and major medical plans provide benefits if the charges were incurred while the claimant was disabled and within the extended benefit period following termination of his insurance.

The benefits provided during these periods of extended insurance are the same as would have been provided had the losses occurred before the insurance terminated, but no premium is charged for coverage during these periods. These extended insurance provisions provide benefits for losses actually beginning while insurance was in force. Time limitations and the disability requirement are necessary to limit claims to those beginning before the insurance terminated.

Employer Omissions

Master contracts provide that whether the group is contributory or noncontributory the employee becomes insured when he becomes eligible and meets the additional requirements, if any, of the prescribed election for insurance. Failure of the employer to report the addition of the employee to the group does not deprive the employee of his insurance, and this provision has been upheld by court decision.[2] However, unless the master contract provides specifically for automatic insurance, it has been held that the policy actually is not complete for the individual employee, and he does not become insured until his application for insurance is accepted.[3]

Assignment by the Employee

The contracts of most group companies provide that "no assignment of the insurance by the employee shall be valid." However, most companies now make a direct use of assignments in administering hospital, surgical, basic medical, and major medical expense claims. The assignment usually takes the form of directing the insurer to pay benefits directly to the hospital or doctor, with a collateral statement that the insurer is relieved of all liability to the certificate holder to the extent of the benefits paid to the hospital or doctor.

The purpose of this use of assignments is to put the insurance proceeds to their intended use: as a reimbursement to the employee for the costs of medical care. The principal value of the privilege of assigning benefits is that a hospital will accept such assignment in lieu of cash settlement of the

---

[2] *All States Life Insurance Company* v. *Tillman,* 226 Ala. 245, 146 S. 393.

[3] *Malone* v. *Protective Life Insurance Company,* 237 Ala. 640, 188 So. 233; and *National Life and Accident Insurance Company* v. *Bridgeforth,* 220 Ala. 314, 124 So. 886.

bill for the portion that appears to be covered by the insurance. Under the State Surgical Plans the employee's direction to pay surgical benefits is used in conjunction with an agreement by the physician to accept the insurance benefits in full payment of charges, if the employee is within certain eligible income groups.

Procedure When Loss Occurs

Notice of Loss. Most contracts require that written notice of sickness or injury must be given to the insurer within twenty days after the day such sickness or injury occurred. The contract includes a definition of date of occurrence for each type of coverage. For income reimbursement it is the first day of absence from work; for hospital expense it is the date of hospital confinement; for accidental death and dismemberment it is the date of the loss; and for other covers it is the date expenses are first incurred.

Contracts provide that failure to give notice within twenty days does not invalidate nor reduce any claim, if it can be shown that it was not reasonably possible to give such notice and that notice was given as soon as reasonably possible. The purpose of such a provision is obvious: claims must be reported within a reasonable time to make efficient and satisfactory claim administration possible. The simplest way to do this is to establish a definite time within which claim notices must be filed. Such a time limit could not be enforced rigidly without injustice to claimants when circumstances prevented giving notice, so some flexibility is necessary to allow for unusual circumstances. This flexibility takes the form of providing an indefinite extension of the time limit, but places the burden of securing the extension upon the person who is to benefit from it.

Some contracts do not require notice by any particular time. The assumption underlying this apparent liberality is that the claimant's desire for benefits will induce him to give notice as soon as it is reasonably possible.

Proof of Loss. Most contracts require that written proof of loss must be furnished to the insurer within ninety days after the date of an accidental death or dismemberment loss, and within ninety days after the termination of the benefit period for other covers.

The contract provides that the insurer must furnish forms for proof of loss to the policyholder. If these forms are not furnished before the expiration of fifteen days after the insurer receives notice of any claim under the policy, the person making the claim is considered to have complied with the policy requirements as to proof of loss upon submitting written proof covering the occurrence, character, and extent of the loss for which claim is made. It is to the insurer's advantage to have proofs of loss filed uniformly in the interest of economical claims administration. The problem of providing forms to secure this uniformity is quite properly one for the insurer.

Right of Examination. The insurer reserves the right to examine the person of the claimant as often as necessary during a pending claim, and in case of death, the right to make an autopsy if it is not prohibited by law. The right to examine the person of an insured individual may be essential to establish the fact that a loss has occurred which is covered by insurance. In the case of death, an autopsy may be the only means of determining the probable cause.

Most companies reserve the right to an autopsy only for the accidental death cover and reserve the right to examination only for accidental death, income reimbursement, basic medical, and major medical covers. For hospital and surgical expense, these companies apparently feel that there is nothing to be gained by reserving a right to examine a claimant.

Payment of Claims. Master contracts specify when claim payments will be made. Benefits that run over a period of time are usually paid weekly or every two weeks, and single benefits or remaining balances of benefits due are paid immediately upon receipt of proof of loss.

Beneficiary Designation

The only insurance cover to which a beneficiary designation is applicable is accidental death and dismemberment. The contract may provide that any employee, while insured under the policy, may from time to time change the beneficiary without the consent of any previously designated beneficiary by filing a written request with the company at its home office. The contract may provide that the change take effect either when the request is signed or when it is received at the home office of the insurer.[4]

Some contracts provide for a succession of beneficiaries and payments to minors when no legal guardian has been appointed. The payment to minors and preference beneficiary provisions apply to accidental death and dismemberment insurance, a part, but not all, of the "facility of payment" clauses common to group life and industrial insurance.

MISCELLANEOUS CONTRACT PROVISIONS

The Contract

The master contract outlines requirements of the contract and the applications for insurance. All statements made by the employer or by the individual employees shall, in the absence of fraud, be deemed representations and not warranties, and no such statement shall void the policy or be used in defense of a claim under the policy unless it is contained in a written application. The majority of group contracts provide that no agent has authority to change the policy or waive any of its provisions and that no change in the policy may be effected without written consent of the company.

---

[4] Notwithstanding the policy provision, it has been held that a change takes effect where the employee had done all in his power to make the change. See *Johnson* v. *Kearns,* 107 Cal. App. 557, 290 Pac. 640; *Koch* v. *Aetna Life Ins. Co.,* 165 Wash. 329, 5 Pac. (2d) 313; *Goodrich* v. *Equitable Life Assurance Society,* 197 N.W. 380 (1924); *Johnson* v. *Johnson,* 139 F. (2d) 930, 151 A. L. R. 268.

Policy Face

The initial page of any insurance contract is customarily called the "face" of the policy, and this page in a group health master contract contains very little besides identification of the parties to the contract, statements concerning the nature of the insurance provided, the policy date and anniversary, and the consideration for the insurance. Since it is customary to include the signatures of the validating company officers only once in a given contract, the first page of the contract may carry a statement to the effect that the provisions of the subsequent pages of the contract form a part of the contract as fully as if recited at length over the validating signatures. The insurer and employer (or other policyholder if not an employer group) are identified in a statement that provides that the insurer will pay the specified benefits to the covered employees in accordance with and subject to the policy provisions.

Changes in Amounts of Insurance

Since the amounts of insurance for individual employees are determined by conditions pertaining to employment, the master contract must make provision for changes in amounts of insurance when employees change classifications. The usual provision states that a change in amount of an employee's personal or dependent insurance takes place on the date of his change in classification. However, if the employee is not actively at work on the date of his change of classification, the change in amount of insurance takes place on his return to active work. On contributory plans the change in amounts of insurance is accompanied by the necessary adjustments on employees' contributions.

Addition of New Employees

The master contract establishes the conditions under which new employees or new members of the organization will be added to the group or classes eligible for insurance. The eligibility of individual employees is usually defined in terms of a minimum number of hours worked per week, satisfaction of a probationary period, and a requirement that the employee be actively at work. Employees whose normal work week calls for a schedule of less than thirty hours usually are not eligible, according to the standards established by most group companies. The usual probationary period is three months of service, but an employer may make a written election with the insurer that previous service of an employee who is re-employed will be counted toward the probationary period. However, an employee who is not actively at work when he would otherwise become eligible for insurance does not become eligible until he returns to active work. The broad purpose of these three phases of the eligibility requirement is to restrict the insurance to full-time, regular or nontransient, and active employees.

Legal Proceedings

The contract provides that no action at law or in equity shall be brought to recover on the policy prior to the expiration of sixty days after proof of loss has been filed in accordance with policy requirements, and that no action shall be brought unless brought within two years from the expiration of the time within which proof of loss is required by the policy. If there is no time limit for proofs of loss, contracts usually provide that actions must be brought within two years and ninety days after the cause of loss arose. All contracts provide that, if any time limitation in the policy with respect to bringing action on the policy is less than that permitted by the laws governing such limitation, the limitation is extended to agree with the minimum period permitted by such laws.

CHAPTER IV

HEALTH INSURANCE LEGISLATION

DURING and after World War II there has been an increasing interest on the part of both state and national legislators in providing various forms of compulsory health insurance. Legislative activity in the states has centered around compulsory nonoccupational income reimbursement insurance, although benefit patterns and methods of insuring have not been at all uniform. Federal legislative activity has covered the entire range of insurance for the disability hazard.

STATE NONOCCUPATIONAL DISABILITY LAWS

One of the most important single events affecting the development of group health insurance has been the adoption in four states of compulsory nonoccupational income reimbursement insurance.[1] The four states having such laws in effect are Rhode Island, California, New Jersey, and New York.[2] A similar law was enacted in the State of Washington but was defeated in a referendum vote on November 7, 1950, by 440,491 to 184,017.[3]

The four state laws now in effect fall into three general classes, according to the manner in which employee benefits

---

[1] For a comprehensive treatment of these laws, see Grant Osborn, *Compulsory Temporary Disability Insurance* (Homewood, Ill.: Richard D. Irwin, Inc., 1958).

[2] Unless otherwise cited, references in this section are to the amended versions of the California Unemployment Compensation Disability Benefits Law, New Jersey Temporary Disability Benefits Law, New York Disability Benefits Law, and Rhode Island Temporary Disability Insurance Act.

[3] *Weekly Underwriter,* November 18, 1950, p. 1143.

are to be insured. Except for Rhode Island, the laws provide only for nonoccupational insurance coverage in the same sense that most voluntary group health insurance is nonoccupational.

In the first class of state laws is Rhode Island, where benefits are provided by a monopolistic state fund. Employers have no opportunity to provide the insurance for employees through private insurance companies.

New Jersey and California fall into the second class of compulsory state laws. In both states employers are automatically covered under the state fund unless they elect to insure with an insurance company or to self-insure.

Under the New York law employers have no automatic coverage under the state fund. The employer is held responsible for providing self-insurance, coverage under the state fund, or insurance with a private insurance company. New York benefits are part of the workmen's compensation law, while the other three are administered as parts of the unemployment compensation laws.

Rhode Island Temporary Disability Insurance

The first compulsory state disability benefit law became effective in Rhode Island in 1943, with the benefits to be provided from the first by a monopolistic state insurance fund.

A waiting period of seven days of disability is required for each benefit year, and the maximum period of benefits is twenty-six weeks, with benefits due to pregnancy limited to twelve weeks. Depending upon past earnings, benefits range from $10 to $36 a week for the disabled employee plus $3 for each dependent up to a maximum of $12 a week for all dependents. Benefits are payable regardless of the cause of loss, and disabled employees may receive benefits from both Workmen's Compensation and Disability Insurance, although maximum combined benefits are limited to 85 per cent of the employee's average wage and can in no event exceed $62, plus benefits for dependents.

Rhode Island benefits are financed by a tax on individual employees of 1 per cent of the first $3,600 of each employee's annual earnings. Since the benefits are provided by a state fund, private group income reimbursement insurance has virtually ceased to exist in Rhode Island, except where employers voluntarily provide insurance in addition to the statutory benefits.

California Unemployment Compensation Disability Benefits

California adopted a compulsory temporary disability benefit law in 1946. An employee is eligible for benefits commencing with the first day of any hospital confinement, but a waiting period of seven days for each disability is required if the employee is not confined to a hospital. The maximum period of benefits is twenty-six weeks, and no benefits are provided for disability due to pregnancy until after twenty-eight days from the termination of the pregnancy.

Benefits range from $10 to $65 a week, depending on past earnings, and employees are entitled to a hospital benefit of $12 a day for not more than twenty days of hospital confinement for each disability. These benefits are financed by a tax on employees of 1 per cent of the first $3,600 of annual wages.

Comparison of Rhode Island and California Laws

There are two important differences between the California and Rhode Island laws. First, there is no duplication of workmen's compensation benefits in California, while in Rhode Island there is at least a partial application of the cover to purely occupational causes. In California a worker is not eligible for disability income benefits during any period for which workmen's compensation benefits (other than benefits for a prior permanent disability) are paid or payable, unless workmen's compensation is less than the disability benefit. In the last case the difference is payable by the nonoccupational disability plan.

Second, a California employer may provide the insurance for his employees through an approved private plan in lieu of insurance under the state plan, if a majority of his employees consent to the private plan. To obtain approval of a private plan, the employer must provide benefits greater in at least one respect than those provided under the state plan, employee contributions may not exceed those under the state plan, and approval of the plan may not result in substantial adverse selection against the state plan. To prevent adverse selection against the state plan, the early California Administrative Code required that 20 per cent of the employees covered by any insurance company must be females. However, this requirement has been suspended for the years 1954 through 1961.

New Jersey Temporary Disability Benefits Law

In 1948 New Jersey adopted a compulsory temporary disability benefit law to become effective January 1, 1949. The maximum benefit is $35 weekly, and minimum amounts and the maximum period of benefits are essentially the same as those of California. No hospital benefits are provided under the New Jersey law, and there is a waiting period of seven days for disability income benefits, regardless of prior hospitalization. Employees are not eligible for benefits during any period for which workmen's compensation benefits are paid or payable, other than benefits for a permanent disability previously incurred.

Employers in New Jersey may choose between the state plan or a private plan, but employees may not be required to contribute more than their contributions would be under the state plan. Under the state plan the rate of employee contribution is 0.5 per cent of the first $3,000 of annual wages, and employers are required to make an initial contribution of 0.25 per cent of each employee's taxable wage. To prevent adverse selection against the state plan because of competition, the employer's contribution to the state plan is subject to experience rating.

New York Disability Benefits Law

In 1949 the trend away from monopolistic state funds was continued in the enactment of the New York Compulsory

Temporary Disability Benefit Law which became effective July 1, 1950. Benefits provided by the New York law are 50 per cent of the base period weekly wage, with a maximum of $50 a week and a minimum of $20 a week or the average wage, whichever is less. The maximum benefit period is twenty-six weeks following a waiting period of one week. Employees are not eligible for benefits during any period in which workmen's compensation benefits are paid or payable, other than permanent partial disability benefits for a prior disability.

The state fund established in New York is unlike that of California and New Jersey, since the New York fund operates as another insurance company in competition with private companies. The employer who wishes to be insured in the state fund must take positive action, just as if he were insuring with a private carrier.

The New York program is partially financed by an employee contribution of 0.5 per cent of the first $60 of weekly wages for statutory benefits. Employee maximum contributions are graded upward from this thirty cent maximum according to the level of benefits, if a private plan provides higher benefits than the statutory. The employer is required to contribute the amount over employee contributions necessary to provide the benefits.

Employers Covered

Each of the four state laws defines employers to be covered in terms of number of employees or the number of employees and the amount of payroll. The definition of employers covered in all four states follows closely the definitions of those covered under unemployment insurance. The California law applies to employers of one or more employees with a payroll of $100 or more in a calendar quarter. The New Jersey law applies to employers of four or more employees in twenty weeks in a calendar year. The New York law applies to employers of one or more employees in thirty days in a calendar year. The Rhode Island law applies to employers of one or more employees on any day.

Benefits for Disabled Unemployed

In Rhode Island, unemployed persons are entitled to disability benefits on the same basis as employed workers. In California, if a disability occurs within three months after a person becomes unemployed or registered at a public employment office, the disabled person is entitled to disability benefits, providing he is eligible otherwise.

In both New York and New Jersey, the employer's disability insurance coverage is extended for a period after termination of employment. In New Jersey, employees becoming disabled within two weeks after termination of employment are entitled to disability benefits from the employer's plan with the private carrier or state fund. In New York, the extended insurance period is four weeks.

After termination of the extended insurance period, employees in New York, New Jersey, and California are covered for unemployment disability benefits under special state funds. New York unemployed workers are eligible for benefits if the disability occurs within twenty-six weeks from termination of employment.

California and New Jersey employees are covered for disability benefits if the disability arises during the unemployment benefit period. Although disability and unemployment benefits are not payable at the same time, both can be received during the same benefit year. However, the New Jersey law provides that the total of such benefits may not exceed one and one-half times the total amount of benefits receivable for either unemployment or disability.

In California, New Jersey, and New York, unemployment disability benefits are financed by assessments where necessary. In California, the assessment is against all plans and is limited to 0.03 per cent of taxable wages to make up any deficit of costs over the interest on the $132 million initial fund for unemployed disability benefits. New Jersey assessments are also against the state fund and private plan employers and are limited to 0.02 per cent of taxable wages to make up the deficit of costs over interest on the initial fund of $50 million. New York assessments are against the insurer of a plan and are not limited as to amount, but are based on the extent to which the fund falls below its original amount of $12 million.

Relation of Benefits to Wages

Within the minimum and maximum amounts prescribed in the particular law, the benefits in all state plans are related to wages in a base pay period. In New York and New Jersey, the wage base period is the last eight weeks of covered employment. In California, the wage base period is the first four of the last five quarters, with benefits related to the "high-quarter" earnings during the base period. In Rhode Island, benefits are related to "high-quarter" earnings during the calendar year preceding the worker's benefit year.

The important difference between the base period used in New York and New Jersey and the "high-quarter" base is that, under the latter, benefits may be related to a wage base considerably out of date. This time lag is not serious in times of rising wages because the premiums are based on current earnings and the base period quarter used will probably be the most recent quarter of the period. However, during periods of falling wages, current benefits may be related to high previous wages, while current premiums are related to current lower wages.

Qualification of Private Plans

In California, New Jersey, and New York, private insurance plans that qualify may be substituted for the statutory plan. To qualify in California, a private plan must be better than the state plan in at least one respect. In New Jersey, private plans must be equal to the state plan; in New York, they must be "at least as favorable" as the state plan.

The original purpose of allowing qualification of plans not meeting exactly the letter of the laws was to avoid disturbing plans in existence on the effective dates of the compulsory disability laws. The New York law is much more flexible than the others in this respect, since plans with less than statutory weekly benefit amounts can meet the requirements of the law by providing health benefits that are the actuarial equivalent of the state plans.

The New York Workmen's Compensation Board has established a scale of values to give credit for income reimbursement policies with more liberal maximum period or waiting period provisions than those of the statutory policies. Credit is also allowed for covers other than accident and sickness, but weekly benefits must be at least 60 per cent of the statutory income reimbursement benefits.

There is considerable merit to the New York practice of allowing new plans to qualify with a variety of benefits. If an employer has only a limited amount to spend for group insurance, the employees' interests may be better served by taking a less liberal income reimbursement plan in conjunction with some form of medical care insurance.

Advantages Claimed for Private Plans

In addition to the possible advantage of having a variety of benefits, there are other practical reasons for choosing private plans. First, an employer can provide more complete group insurance at lower administration cost by purchasing life and health insurance in a "package" from an insurance carrier. Second, the maximum statutory benefits are somewhat low compared with levels of benefits currently being sought by both union and nonunion employees. Again, it is less expensive to provide benefits under a single policy than to have two insurance policies with duplication of costs and claim procedures. Third, employers with multiple locations can secure a private plan providing the same benefits to employees in all locations, or the plan can be made flexible to meet economic conditions prevailing in the different locations. Fourth, the larger employers may secure greater dividends or rate reductions under a package arrangement with a single insurer, because of the greater credibility of experience than would be found under a variety of policies with lower individual premiums.

Impact of State Laws on Group Health Insurance

One of the most important immediate results of the state laws was to focus attention on providing group health insurance for small groups. Insurance for small groups had never been actively solicited for two main reasons: first, underwriters had some misgivings about the possibilities of adverse selection by groups under a rate system which would need to recognize high expense ratios; second, the sales force had paid relatively little attention to small groups because of the low potential earnings per case. In retrospect, neither of these reasons appears to have been sound.

The state laws have had a direct effect on company underwriting results, but the result has not been the same in states where companies are permitted to write qualifying plans.

Rhode Island. Private companies were virtually put out of the income reimbursement business automatically in Rhode Island because employers were blanketed into the state fund. Since employers are required to insure with the state fund, the only group income reimbursement insurance private companies can write is coverage in excess of statutory benefits.

New York. The most favorable underwriting results have been achieved in New York. There are two broad reasons for this relatively successful underwriting picture.

First, the New York law permitted a minimum of disturbance of established benefit plans and underwriting rules through plan qualification with a variety of benefits. Of the total taxable payroll in 1954 of $12,144,085,487, there was $4,119,586,165 (33.92 per cent) applicable to "precisely" statutory coverage, and an additional $1,597,593,198 (13.15 per cent) applicable to "substantially" statutory coverage.[4] These leave almost 53 per cent of covered payroll applicable to nonstatutory benefits. The "precisely" and "substantially" statutory coverage have produced claim costs for 1951–54 of 0.31 per cent of covered

---

[4] From figures released by the New York Insurance Department, May 26, 1955, and from Bureau of Accident and Health Underwriters, *New York Release No. 164*, p. 1.

payrolls,[5] and with estimated premiums running at about 0.5 per cent of payrolls, loss ratios were about 60 per cent.

For all plans combined in New York, the earned premiums (after payment of experience refunds) under private plans exceeded losses and expenses incurred in all years through 1956, but the companies had a combined ratio of losses and expenses incurred to earned premiums (after experience refunds) of 104.1 per cent in 1957.[6]

The second important reason for the relatively successful underwriting picture in New York is the relationship between private insurers and the state fund. There was no automatic blanketing of employers into the state fund, and the state fund pays premium taxes as any private carrier does. Because the state fund receives no "automatic" business, it has acquisition costs comparable to those for other carriers. All carriers in New York, including the state fund, charge a "premium" for benefits although there is a fixed maximum employee contribution. This means that the state fund receives no automatic competitive advantage when statutory benefits are increased, because the state fund has approximately the same claims and expense problems as private carriers.

California.   Underwriting results of private insurers in California have been poor almost from the beginning for two reasons. First, employers were automatically blanketed into the state fund unless they elected a private plan with "greater" benefits than the statutory plan and with employee contributions no greater than those required under the statutory plan. This blanketing of course meant that private carriers were forced to "sell" employers on electing a private plan (with attendant acquisition costs not in effect for the state fund) and on paying any additional cost that might be required for the "greater" benefit feature, since employee contributions are the same under either. Private insurers are required to pay

---

[5] New York Insurance Department Release, May 26, 1955. The figures by years for the period were: 1951, 0.29 per cent; 1952, 0.30 per cent; 1953, 0.32 per cent, and 1954, 0.31 per cent.

[6] Life Insurance Association of America, *Group Insurance and Group Annuity Manual,* Vol. I, "Cash Sickness," p. 11. (For the remainder of this chapter this source will be cited LIAA.)

premium taxes, but these are not applicable to the state fund.

The second reason for poor results in California is a logical outgrowth of the first. Blanketing of employers into the state fund and freedom from acquisition costs and premium taxes give the state fund a very low expense rate and thus room for a relatively high loss ratio under a given employee contribution rate. Loss ratios (including regular benefit payments and net unemployment disability payments, after private plan assessments) rose from 34.42 per cent in 1947 to 79.76 per cent in 1953.[7] Benefit increases were the logical result when the state fund was showing favorable underwriting results, and each of the periodic increases in benefits put more pressure on private insurer rate levels with attendant loss of more and more groups to the state fund. After January 1, 1954, when weekly benefits were increased from $30 to $35 and the hospital benefit from $8 to $10, there was a considerable shift of business to the state fund. By June 30, 1954, the number of employees under private plans and the number of private plans both were 10 per cent below the 1953 figures.[8] Voluntary plans in 1953 applied to 50.1 per cent of all covered employees, but this had dropped to 42.1 per cent by 1958.[9]

The benefit increases of January 1, 1954, prompted one group underwriter to state, ". . . one more round of increased benefits and the State will have all the business."[10] In spite of all their troubles, voluntary plans in California produced an underwriting profit from 1955 to 1957, but there was a small underwriting loss in 1958.[11]

New Jersey. Although benefit levels have not been raised as frequently or as much in New Jersey as in California, the

---

[7] California Department of Employment, *Report 1009, No. 9,* February 2, 1954, Table 1.

[8] California Department of Employment, *Report 1006A, No. 5,* March 25, 1955, p. 1.

[9] LIAA, *op. cit.,* p. 26.

[10] W. Walter Mincks, "Trend in Loss of Time Coverages," address at Educational Seminar, Bureau of Accident and Health Underwriters, February 2 and 3, 1954.

[11] LIAA, *op. cit.,* p. 28.

factors affecting private insurer success are potentially the same. The New Jersey system blankets employers into the state fund, and private insurers have acquisition costs where the state fund does not. Fifty-nine insurance companies writing New Jersey benefits in 1953 had losses, dividends, and expenses of $188,406.74 more than earned premiums.[12]

Estimates of employees covered under private plans and the state plan were 927,406 and 499,780 respectively on January 1, 1955,[13] but the corresponding figures were 906,190 and 521,000 on April 1, 1955.[14] During 1954, 1,146 private plans were terminated and 948 approved, and while some of those terminated were simply changes to new plans, a large number were terminated because of rate increases.[15]

The sixty-one insurance companies writing New Jersey benefits in 1955 had earned premiums that exceeded losses, dividends, and expenses by $1,206,341.52.[16] The October 1, 1955 increase in maximum benefit to $35, without an increase in the employee contribution rate, did not lead to a general rate increase by private companies, because the underwriting results in 1955 were acceptable. Consequently, the January, 1957 ratio of private plan coverage to state plan coverage remained about the same as the ratio in 1955.[17] However, insured private plans produced underwriting losses during 1956 and 1957 of $85 million and $794 million respectively.[18]

Legislative Activity in Other States

A number of bills have been introduced at each session of various state legislatures, but 1951 was the year with the most activity. During 1951 thirty-six compulsory disability bills were

---

[12] New Jersey Department of Labor and Industry, Division of Employment Security, *Eighteenth Annual Employment Security Report,* January, 1955, p. 47.

[13] *Ibid.,* p. 51.

[14] Bureau of Accident and Health Underwriters, *Bulletin No. 92,* April 27, 1955.

[15] New Jersey Department of Labor and Industry, *op. cit.,* p. 49.

[16] New Jersey Department of Labor and Industry, Division of Employment Security, *Twentieth Annual Employment Security Report,* January, 1957, p. 68.

[17] *Ibid.,* p. 59.

[18] LIAA, *op. cit.,* p. 19.

introduced in fourteen states, but none of the bills was passed.[19]

Since there are three different types of laws among the four state laws now in existence, there is considerable speculation as to what the future will bring in the field of compulsory accident and sickness legislation. It has been stated that "if this trend were to continue, the natural reaction would be for one (federal) system."[20] Others have believed that state adoption of plans would prevent a national system of income reimbursement coverage. Individual states developed their heterogeneous workmen's compensation laws, which have not been supplanted by a federal system, but this historical example is not strictly analogous to the nonoccupational disability field. A type of insurance in which employees are required to bear all or a part of the costs creates an entirely different political atmosphere.

FEDERAL HEALTH LEGISLATION

Many proposals for providing income reimbursement and medical expense reimbursement have been introduced in both houses of Congress in recent years. Although most of these were reintroduced year after year in slightly modified form, there is as yet no national system of medical care insurance, although some segments of the population have been provided with benefits. Income reimbursement benefits are provided by both the Railroad Unemployment Insurance Act and the Old Age, Survivors, and Disability Insurance Act.

Both the existing plans which involve substantial numbers of persons and the proposed plans are discussed and classified below according to the nature of the benefits and the methods of providing benefits.

Income Reimbursement Benefits

The Social Security (OASDI) Act was amended in 1956 to provide total disability retirement benefits to eligible workers

[19] These states were Arizona, Connecticut, Florida, Illinois, Indiana, Maryland, Massachusetts, Minnesota, Nevada, New Hampshire, New Mexico, Ohio, West Virginia, and Wisconsin. *National Underwriter,* September 19, 1951, p. 39.

[20] E. H. O'Connor, "Legislative Trends," *Group Proceedings of the Health and Accident Underwriters Conference,* 1952, p. 39.

under the Act, but these benefits could not be paid until the worker reached age 50. Coverage was broadened in 1958, and the age restriction was removed in 1960.[21] The discussion below will be based on coverage provisions as they exist after the 1960 amendments.

Eligibility Requirements. To be eligible for benefits, a worker must meet four requirements. First, he must have earned twenty quarters of coverage during the forty calendar quarters just prior to the quarter in which he became disabled. Second, the worker must be "fully insured," and this means that he must have earned one quarter (at any time) for each three quarters that expire after 1950 (or after the year he reached age 21, if later than 1950) up to the year of his disability. The third requirement is that the worker must be so disabled that he is unable to "engage in any substantial gainful activity," and he must remain so disabled for a period of six months before eligibility for benefits. The fourth requirement is that the disability must be expected to continue for a long and indefinite time.

Benefits. The amount of benefit payable is the same as that provided for retirement and is figured from the worker's average wage during the period of work with which he is charged. The maximum monthly benefit to the worker is $127, and the maximum monthly benefit to an entire family is $254.

The benefits are payable to each of the following persons: (1) the disabled worker; (2) his dependent child or children under age 18; (3) a dependent child or children age 18 or over who become totally disabled before age 18; (4) wife, regardless of age, if she is caring for a child eligible for benefits; (5) wife age 62 or over; and (6) a dependent husband age 65 or over.

Earnings of more than $1,200 during a year by a dependent will disqualify that dependent for some benefits, but there is no effect on the benefits of the eligible worker or other dependents. A disabled worker who recovers from his disability

---

[21] P.L. 778, 86th Cong., 2d sess.

is entitled to benefits for three months after the recovery, and he may receive benefits for twelve months under a special trial work provision. A disabled worker who reaches retirement age is automatically changed from a disability to a retired status.

Proposed Changes. Early in 1961 President Kennedy proposed an amendment to the OASDI Act, not only to liberalize benefits, but to stimulate the economy by placing additional money in the hands of several million people. The proposal, introduced in the House of Representatives,[22] would make the following changes: (1) increase the minimum benefit to a worker from $33 to $43 per month; (2) lower the retirement age for men to age 62, with reduced benefits, as it is now for women; (3) lower the requirements for fully insured status to one in four quarters instead of the present one in three; (4) increase the benefit amount of elderly widows and widowers to 85 per cent of the worker's primary insurance amount, instead of the present 75 per cent; and (5) liberalize the disability benefit requirement by removing the requirement that the disability must appear to be permanent.

The cost of the benefits under the proposal would be financed by an increase in the present tax scale of 0.25 per cent for both the employer and the employee, with the increase to become effective January 1, 1963.

Medical Expense Reimbursement Benefits

Plans have been adopted during the last few years which provide benefits for dependents of members of the uniformed services, for federal employees and their dependents, and assistance to states in helping the needy elderly.

Uniformed Services Program for Dependents. The program for dependents of servicemen became effective December 7, 1956.[23] Since 1884, dependents of servicemen on active duty have been eligible for medical care in government facilities "whenever practicable." Such services are still available, but P.L. 569, generally referred to as "Medicare," pro-

---

[22] H.R. 4571, 87th Cong.
[23] P.L. 569, 84th Cong., 2d sess.

vides dependents of servicemen with a broad range of coverage for expenditures in civilian facilities.

Civilian medical care coverage is provided to the following dependents of a servicemen on active duty for a period exceeding thirty days: (1) lawful wife; (2) legitimate child, including an adopted child or stepchild, under 21 years of age; (3) legitimate child under age 23 and unmarried who is taking a full-time course of study at a recognized college, if dependent on the serviceman for more than one half of his support; (4) unmarried legitimate child over age 21 who is dependent because of mental or physical incapacity suffered before age 21; and (5) lawful husband who is dependent for more than one half his support.

Medical services are available in service facilities only, to certain classes of dependents. These are: (1) widows and dependent children, if death of the serviceman occurred while on active duty or retired; (2) parents and parents-in-law, if dependent upon the serviceman and living in his household; and (3) an unremarried widower who was dependent on the deceased for more than one half his support due to mental or physical disability.

Benefits provided in civilian facilities under Medicare cover a broad range of hospital, outpatient, surgical, and medical charges. Hospital semiprivate accommodations (as defined locally) are provided up to 365 days for each admission, subject to a deductible of the greater of $25 or $1.75 per day. When the physician certifies that private accommodations are required, the plan pays 75 per cent of the excess over an average semiprivate cost.

Surgery charges are paid in full, as are in-hospital doctors' charges and maternity charges. For special nurses ordered by the physician, the plan pays 75 per cent of the excess over $100.

The plan is not all-inclusive in its coverage, and the following diseases or charges are not covered: (1) chronic ailments, except for acute attacks and resulting complications requiring hospitalization; (2) elective medical or surgical care; (3) nervous and mental disorders, except acute emergencies requiring hospitalization; (4) domiciliary care only; (5) ambulance service; and (6) outpatient care not involving bodily injury.

In its operation Medicare is handled by private carriers in midwestern and southeastern United States, and the West and East are serviced by Blue Cross and Blue Shield. These carriers serve as fiscal agents for the government on a cost-plus basis, and they pay benefits directly to the hospitals and doctors.

Federal Employees Plan. The Federal Employees Health Benefits Act of 1959 became effective in July, 1960.[24] This act provided for a contributory plan of insurance for federal employees and their dependents covering a wide range of basic hospital and medical charges, plus extended or major medical coverage.

Employees are permitted to make a selection of coverage from four types of plans, with each type carrying a further option of two levels of benefit. The four general types of plan available are: (1) a government-wide service plan administered by Blue Cross and Blue Shield; (2) a government-wide indemnity (private carrier) plan provided by a number of insurance companies and administered by the Aetna Life Insurance Company; (3) an employee organization plan for members of the organization only, underwritten and administered by the organization itself in some cases and by private carriers in others; and (4) a comprehensive medical plan on the group practice or individual practice prepayment basis in geographical areas where such plans are available.

Since there is such a variety of plans and costs in all plans except the two government-wide plans, it does not seem feasible to discuss any plans in this chapter except the latter two. Accordingly, a brief summary of the benefits of the Blue Cross and Indemnity plans will be discussed below.

The Blue Cross hospital coverage, under the "high option," provides for full coverage in member hospitals of the daily room charge for semiprivate care, and hospital extras for a

---

[24] P.L. 382, 86th Cong., 1st sess.

period of 120 days each hospital admission. In nonmember hospitals the benefit for the daily room charge is limited to $12, and the plan pays 90 per cent of the charges for hospital extras.

Benefits for surgery and physicians' services under Blue Shield are set by a benefit schedule, and the patient must pay the excess if he lives in a "nonservice area" or uses a non-participating doctor in a "service area." Parts or all of thirty-two states and all areas outside the United States are nonservice areas. In the service areas, participating physicians agree to accept the scheduled benefit in full settlement of the charge, if income is under $4,000 a year for an individual or $6,000 for an employee with dependents.

Maternity benefits are provided by the plan, up to $100 for hospital charges and a scheduled benefit for the obstetrician and anesthetist.

A supplemental plan over basic provides for payment of 80 per cent of the excess over a $100 out-of-pocket deductible, up to a maximum per individual of $20,000.

The "low option" plan at a lower premium rate provides the same type of coverage, but it has a limit on hospital benefits of thirty days, a lower fee schedule, and a $200 deductible on the supplemental plan, along with only a 75 per cent payment on the excess up to a maximum of $5,000 per person.

The private carrier plan, under its "high option," pays the first $1,000 of hospital room and board charges for semiprivate care during each calendar year and 80 per cent of any charge over that amount. For other hospital charges, surgery, and physicians' services, the indemnity plan pays 80 per cent of the excess over a $50 calendar year deductible. Maternity benefits are provided by the plan up to 10 days of hospital care at $15 per day, and a scheduled amount is paid for the obstetrician and anesthetist. The maximum benefit per person under the indemnity plan is $30,000.

The "low option" indemnity plan provides a maximum benefit of $10,000 per person. This plan is limited to paying the first $250 of hospital room and board charges per calendar year and 75 per cent of the excess. Following the $50 deductible applicable to hospital extras, surgery, and physicians' charges, the plan pays 75 per cent of the excess. Maternity benefits are limited to two thirds of the scheduled dollar amounts provided by the "high option" plan.

For all four general types of plans and for both options under each type, the government makes the same contribution on behalf of the employee and the employee pays the balance of the cost by payroll deduction. The 1961 monthly contributions by the government are shown in the following exhibit:

Employee only	$2.82
Employee and family	6.76
Female employee and family, with nondependent husband	3.94

If coverage under any plan terminates other than by voluntary termination of coverage, it can be converted without evidence of insurability to individual plans currently offered by the insuring carrier. Renewal of the converted policy of any employee or dependent can be refused only for reasons of fraud, overinsurance, or nonpayment of premiums.

Grants-in-Aid to States. The 1960 amendments to the Federal Old Age, Survivors, and Disability Insurance Act provided for an increase in aid to states for providing added medical care for the needy aged.[25] Two changes in the previous aid provision were made. First, the federal government will assume an increased responsibility with respect to sharing the costs of medical expenditures by those who are on the old age assistance rolls of the states. Second, federal aid will be supplied so that states may provide assistance in meeting medical costs of those not on old age assistance rolls but not able to pay for their own medical care.

The federal portion of this additional aid will range from 50 to 80 per cent, and it will be determined by a formula based primarily on per capita income in the state.

---

[25] P.L. 778, 86th Cong., 2d sess.

Federal Health Insurance Proposals

Federal health insurance plans discussed in the preceding section are those which have been adopted, but there have been numerous other proposals made in the last decade which have not been adopted. These proposals have included such approaches as national compulsory health insurance, voluntary insurance with federal insurance of low income families, voluntary insurance with federal reinsurance of private plans, modifications of income tax rules on medical costs, and the addition of medical care benefits to the OASDI program. Many of these are now largely of historical interest only, so the discussion below will deal only with the reinsurance proposal and the proposed addition of medical care benefits to OASDI.

Federal Reinsurance.   Federal reinsurance of private plans was the approach favored after 1955 by the Eisenhower administration. The 1955 proposals followed the pattern of earlier proposals by continuing to recognize voluntary plans of both private insurers and nonprofit organizations.[26] Under these, voluntary plans would have to meet requirements to be laid down by the Department of Health, Education and Welfare to qualify for reinsurance. Liability of the reinsurance fund would be limited to 75 per cent of the excess of annual incurred claim costs over the difference between annual earned premiums and an administrative expense allowance. Premium charges for the reinsurance would be fixed as a percentage of each carrier's earned premiums, without allowance for dividends.

A reinsurance system would be useless if the "regulations" provided for in the proposals set rates or qualification requirements at levels which discouraged participation in the plan. The plan at best would solve the problem no better than would a conservative rate and reserve system by the individual companies, since reinsurance in its usual sense is unnecessary in group health insurance. The same factors that inhibit conserva-

---

[26] S. 886, H.R. 400, 401, and 3458, 84th Cong., 1st sess.

tism in rates and reserves would probably inhibit entry into the reinsurance plan.

Addition of Medical Care to Existing Programs. Early in 1961 President Kennedy recommended the amendment of the Railroad Retirement Act and the OASDI Act to provide a broad range of medical benefits for recipients of other benefits under these acts. This recommendation was introduced in both houses of Congress early in the 1961 session.[27] In substance the 1961 proposal follows the much-debated but unsuccessful Forand Bill of the previous Congress.[28]

Medical benefits would be provided in the following general areas: (1) semiprivate hospital care; (2) skilled nursing home services after discharge from a hospital; (3) home health services; and (4) outpatient diagnostic services provided by a hospital.

Semiprivate hospital care would be limited to ninety days for each illness, and a period of ninety days out of hospitals and skilled nursing homes would be required before the patient would be eligible for a new period of benefits. A deductible of $10 a day would be applied, with a minimum deductible of $20. No benefits would be provided for private nurses, and physicians' services in the hospital would be excluded except for pathology, radiology, physiatry, or anesthesiology.

Skilled nursing home services would be provided up to 180 days maximum, but this benefit would be limited to a combination of hospital care and nursing home care of 150 "units of service." Each day in a hospital would count as one unit of service, while two days in a nursing home would make one unit of service. This provision would be an incentive for the patient to use nursing home service if such care would be adequate.

Home health services would be provided up to 240 visits per calendar year when the person is under the care of a physician. This would include nursing care, therapy, and part-time homemaker services.

---

[27] S. 909 and H.R. 4222, 87th Cong.

[28] H.R. 4700, 86th Cong., 1st sess.

Outpatient hospital diagnostic services would be provided as required, but a $20 deductible would be applied to each study.

The 1961 proposal would be financed by raising the taxable wage base to $5,000 on January 1, 1962, and by the addition a year later of an additional 0.25 per cent to the tax rates of both the employer and the employee.

CANADIAN HEALTH INSURANCE PLANS

All the Canadian Provinces (except Quebec) and the two territories have a compulsory, province-wide, medical expense reimbursement plan.[29] All the existing plans provide benefits for standard ward hospital service and for most hospital miscellaneous charges. All plans except that in Alberta provide outpatient services for accidents. All the plans except two provide benefits for as long as "medically necessary." The plan in British Columbia provides benefits as long as the patient is in need of active treatment requiring hospitalization, and the Alberta plan provides benefits while the sickness is in its acute stage.

Medical and surgical benefits are provided through private insurance carriers to some extent, but most of this type of coverage is provided by local (provincial) medical societies, similar in their operations to the Blue Shield plans in the United States. Both Blue Cross and private carriers provide basic and major medical benefits to supplement the state plans.

The coverage is very wide in scope, because the plans are compulsory to all residents in seven of the nine plans. The Ontario plan applies to all employees and dependents of all employers who employ fifteen or more residents. In the Prince Edward Island plan, coverage is compulsory to an employer when the employer, his employees, and their dependents total three or more residents.

---

[29] For an excellent detailed summary of the provisions of these plans, see Health Insurance Association of America, "Student's Guide for Basic Course in Group A & H Insurance," Supplement XII.

Newfoundland and Alberta provide immediate coverage to residents, but the others apply a probationary period measured either from the date of registration or from the date of becoming a resident. These probationary periods range from one month after registration in Manitoba to twelve months of residence in British Columbia.

The plans in Alberta, British Columbia, and Newfoundland are financed from general revenues, without premium payments by covered persons or a specially designated tax. The Nova Scotia plan is financed by a special selective sales tax. The others are financed on a contributory basis, with employees paying up to $50.40 a year per family in Ontario and New Brunswick.

CHAPTER V

THE SELLING OF GROUP HEALTH INSURANCE

THE selling of group health insurance presents many problems to insurers, and each meets these problems in what it considers the most efficient and practical manner. Even though fierce competition exists in the group field, the unofficial trading or borrowing of ideas and procedures and many joint attempts to solve problems have made for considerable uniformity in techniques of different companies. The following discussion will emphasize the usual practices, but an attempt will be made to point out significant variations where they exist.

The sale of group health insurance differs markedly from the sale of individual insurance. In individual insurance each person to be insured will require a separate and complete sales transaction. In group insurance the insurer may be attempting to insure only a few persons or a group including thousands of individuals under a single contract, with selling efforts concentrated on the employer (or other policyholder) and not on the individuals who will ultimately be insured.

It may be said that individuals to be insured must be "sold" the insurance plan if they are to contribute to premiums, but in group insurance this portion of the sales process is ordinarily performed by the policyholder or with his active support, if he is paying part of the premium. The general recognition by employees today of the advantages of group health insurance makes selling in the usual sense unnecessary, especially if there is a bargaining unit to represent the employees. Group insurance is thus characterized by a system of mass sales, regardless of whether sales efforts are to show the advantages of group insurance or are merely to show the advantages of a particular plan or carrier.

METHODS OF SELLING

The group sales of a company may require the services of insurance brokers, agents, and salaried group insurance specialists. The completion of any particular sale may involve all three, as each plays an important part in the group sales process.

Agents

Sales by agents account for the largest portion of all groups written by insurance companies, and life insurance companies commonly depend upon ordinary and industrial agents for the actual sales or at least for prospecting for potential sales. However, agents seldom perform all the functions necessary to complete a sale. Putting the insurance plan into operation requires a great deal of specialized knowledge and a considerable amount of time. Group insurance specialists are ordinarily called in by the agent to perform the enrollment of employees, establish the administration system, and give general help and advice to the agent in the completion of the sale.

Brokers

Insurance brokers account for a smaller number of groups than agents, but they control a large portion of the large groups. This is true primarily because it is common for a large business to select a broker to handle all insurance needs of the business. Group insurance is then only one of the many types of insurance the broker handles for his client.

Brokers perform much the same function as the insurance agent, leaving the handling of details to home office group specialists. A brokerage firm may have personnel specializing in employee benefit plans, or it may deal with company representatives who submit proposals on a group to the brokerage firm for consideration.

Salaried Representatives

Salaried representatives of the home office ordinarily do not originate group insurance sales. Their activities are usually limited to assisting agents in developing and soliciting prospects, installing the plan, and servicing the plan after it is installed. However, most Blue Cross–Blue Shield plans are both sold and serviced by salaried representatives.

COMMISSIONS

Commissions to agents and brokers are based upon the volume of premiums written. Commissions are paid not only on first-year premiums but also on renewal premiums for several years after the first policy year. Where more than one person is responsible for placing the insurance on a given group, companies divide the commissions between them as nearly as possible on the basis of the contribution of each to the actual sale.

Commission scales in use vary by company, but the commission agreements in general recognize two basic principles: (1) rates of commission are higher for first-year premiums than for renewal premiums, since the greatest task of the agent is accomplished when he has convinced the employer of the general advantages of group insurance; and (2) commission rates are relatively higher on groups paying lower total premiums, since the amount of work involved for the agent does not necessarily vary directly with the amount of the premiums.[1] Following these principles, various scales of commissions are currently in use. Table 3 demonstrates a sliding scale of commissions according to premium volume for both initial and renewal premiums.

The commission scale shown in Table 3 is the familiar graded scale used by most life companies, with commissions payable for ten years; but casualty companies usually provide for commissions as long as the group remains insured. The

---

[1] James D. Craig, "Group Health Insurance," *Proceedings, Casualty Actuarial and Statistical Society of America,* Vol. 7 (1920–21), p. 91.

THE SELLING OF GROUP HEALTH INSURANCE   89

maximum commission rate usually paid by casualty companies is 10 per cent, but over a long period commissions may actually aggregate a more substantial sum. The agent generally provides less service to the insurer after the group is written, although continued service may be substantial.

Life companies offer a choice between a level commission for both initial and renewal years and the more usual high

TABLE 3

COMMISSION RATES FOR GROUP HEALTH INSURANCE,
FIRST YEAR AND RENEWAL PREMIUMS

Portion of the Premium to Which Rates Are Applied	Commission Rates for First Policy Year Premiums	Commission Rates for Each of the First Nine Renewal Policy Year Premiums
First $ 1,000	20%	5%
Next 4,000	20	3
Next 5,000	15	1½
Next 10,000	12½	1½
Next 10,000	10	1½
Next 20,000	5	1½
Next 50,000	2½	1

first-year and lower renewal-year rates. The level scale is graded by size of premium also; and where the two scales are offered, they are designed to produce approximately the same total commissions over the life of the ten-year commission pay-ing period. Some life companies apply the level commission scale to all groups transferring from another insurer. This practice is aimed at reducing the temptation to "twist," and it also serves to keep initial expenses lower on groups that might make another transfer at the end of the first year or soon there-after.

TYPES OF GROUPS SOLICITED

Agents are limited in their solicitation of groups by the underwriting rules of their particular companies. Some com-panies permit solicitation of groups with as few as five em-ployees or with the minimum number required by law in the state where the group is located. Many companies require a minimum of twenty-five employees, and some limit solicitation of groups with fewer than fifty employees to very stable groups only. The stability of the group becomes important if the size of the group is close to the required minimum number of employees, because it might be difficult to meet the minimum participation requirements if the employment of the group is seasonal or if labor turnover is high.

Groups that transfer from one insurer to another can pose serious underwriting problems, but there are conflicting attitudes among companies concerning these transfer groups. Many, and perhaps most, companies do not restrict their agents in the solicitation of groups already insured in another company. Because of strong competition, benefit plans and ultimate costs vary little between companies, and a group that is willing to transfer to another insurer usually will do so because of a poor loss record and a threatened rate increase. If the loss record is good, a group will usually find it advantageous to continue a contract already in force rather than undergo the heavy first-year expenses of a new contract.[2]

Those companies that fully recognize the disadvantages to the group and to insurers of transferring business may permit solicitation of insured groups only under limited circumstances. Solicitation may be discouraged by providing that no commissions are payable except for additional employees insured and higher amounts of insurance than were provided by the previous plan. The company may require that the agent make no rate quotation until after the home office staff has studied and evaluated the previous carrier's experience with the group.[3] Some companies apply the rather indefinite rule that no solicitation of an insured group should be made unless there is general dissatisfaction with the existing plan or unless participation in the plan is low.

---

[2] See Chapter VII for a discussion of expense allocation.

[3] Data on this experience are acquired directly from the policyholder. If the company is wary of the group, no quotation will be made prior to receiving information regarding previous experience.

Whatever the rules applied by the more conservative companies, the desire for premium volume is still strong. Even if the previous experience of the group has been consistently bad, an optimistic company can often be found, especially if the group is large.

A company may choose to offer group insurance to all types of groups permitted by state laws or rulings. The most common type of group solicited is the employer group, but group health insurance may be offered also to labor unions, trustee groups, and associations.

Employer Groups

To be eligible for group insurance, an employer may be an individual proprietorship, partnership, or corporation. If the employer is an individual proprietor, the insurance may be issued to cover the proprietor himself if he is actively engaged in the conduct of the business. Partners in a partnership may be considered eligible for insurance if they are actively engaged in the business. Officers of corporations are not eligible for insurance unless they receive a regular stipulated salary for performing services other than the usual duties of a director. Affiliated companies are eligible for a single group contract, and if a parent organization has one or more subsidiaries, any one or all of them may be included under a policy issued to the parent organization, but usually only if the parent organization has direct control of the subsidiary through stock ownership or contract. The personal employees of partners or officers of corporations are not considered employees for insurance purposes.

Labor Unions

Health insurance may be issued to cover the members of a labor union or a local unit of the union, if it meets minimum group requirements. Some of the larger companies do not write insurance to cover unions because of the many underwriting and administrative problems involved. Some of the problems encountered are inherent in groups containing members eligible for insurance who may not be actively at work, and many of the problems arise from the internal organization of the union itself. These problems are discussed in Chapter VIII.

Trustee Groups

In most states group health contracts may be issued to trustees of a fund established by a union and one or more employers, two or more employers in the same industry, one or more unions, or the employer members of a trade association. Some state laws outline in detail the conditions under which such contracts may be issued, but even without legal restrictions the insurer must underwrite such groups carefully. The group must have been formed for some purpose other than obtaining insurance, otherwise selection against the insurer would make group insurance impossible. Minimum participation requirements are imposed, but they vary according to the nature of the group to be insured.

The master contract is issued to the trustees of the fund. The primary purpose of this arrangement is to permit small employers or unions to qualify for group insurance by acting through a single agency for premium remittance and administration. The insurer can keep expenses of administration at a reasonable level by dealing with a trustee empowered to make premium payments from an established fund.

Association Groups

Most states either authorize or do not prohibit the issuance of group health insurance to members of trade associations without the use of a trustee. There are two forms of association group insurance: contracts issued to insure employees of the association members, and contracts issued to insure only proprietors, partners, and executives of the member firms.[4] Many

---

[4] Paul S. Fisher, "Trade and Professional Association Group Insurance," *Proceedings, Group Meeting, Health and Accident Underwriters Conference,* 1951, pp. 47–49.

professional organizations, such as associations of lawyers and doctors, fall in the second category.

Just as in trustee groups, the association must have been formed for some purpose other than obtaining insurance. Many companies will issue association group insurance only if the association is very stable, with low turnover among members and uniformity of occupation among those to be insured. Lodges, fraternities, social clubs, and political groups are considered by most insurers to be so unstable in membership that it would be impossible to avoid serious adverse selection.

Creditor Groups

Income reimbursement insurance for creditors, similar to creditor group life insurance, may provide an insurance benefit to pay credit installments if the debtor is disabled. Benefits are based on the period of disability, and disability need not exist on the due date of an installment. Waiting periods of three, seven, or fourteen days are usually required, but in some plans benefits are retroactive after disability exists a minimum period of time. Benefits are prorated for partial months of disability, since disability need not exist on the installment due date.

The bulk of creditor income reimbursement insurance is still written on an individual policy basis, but with sales handled by the lending institution. Group insurance in the usual sense is attained by some lending institutions, but participation is so low in most that the insurance is franchise rather than group.

TYPES OF INSURANCE SOLD

The types of insurance sold to any group are divided into "primary" and "secondary" covers. The primary covers are those which may be issued alone; the secondary are those which are issued only in conjunction with one or more primary covers. Life insurance, annuities, income reimbursement, hospital expense, and major medical are considered primary covers. Except for special situations, all dependent covers are considered secondary, and under certain conditions employee hospital expense insurance is treated as a secondary cover.[5]

Most companies apply the following rules for issuing secondary covers:

1. Surgical expense insurance is issued only with hospital expense or income reimbursement insurance.

2. Basic medical expense plans are issued only with hospital expense, income reimbursement, or surgical expense insurance. The rules for this type of cover depend on the nature of the benefits provided. Coverage for visits by a physician may be issued in conjunction with income reimbursement and surgery coverage, but coverage for diagnostic procedures is ordinarily issued only with hospital expense insurance.

3. The dread disease or poliomyelitis cover is usually issued only with hospital expense insurance. If it is issued alone or with some other cover, higher rates must be applied.

4. Accidental death and dismemberment insurance is issued only with life, income reimbursement, hospital expense, or major medical insurance.

5. The major medical cover will be issued only with hospital expense insurance, if the cover is designed (and rated) as supplementary to a basic plan. For those plans issued as supplementary to a basic plan written by another carrier, expense loading must be added to treat it as a primary cover.

There are three reasons why the secondary covers may be issued only with some other cover. First, many of the disability lines of insurance are offered as supplementary benefits to the more basic covers. Offering the "fringe" benefit without the broader basic coverage would not be a sound approach to health insurance. Second, premium rates for the secondary covers do not contain sufficient loading to permit them to stand alone. Since the benefits are limited in nature for the frill covers, the pure premium for these would be relatively low, and loading sufficient to pay for separate administration would result in a premium much too high for the benefits provided. Third, adverse selection would result from permitting groups complete freedom in choosing types of benefits.

---

[5] Some companies require that more than one cover be issued if hospital expense benefits are at a high level. This is done to give the insurer a spread of hazard within the package.

The general rules concerning issuance of the secondary covers are usually followed rather carefully, but they may be waived to provide a special service to some particular group. If a group wants some secondary cover to round out an existing program, a company may be willing to underwrite the single cover to have a better opportunity to secure. all the group business later.

COMPETITION BETWEEN PRIVATE CARRIERS AND ASSOCIATION PLANS

Since the beginning of group health insurance, there has been strong competition between private insurance companies and association plans, such as Blue Cross and Blue Shield. Most of this competition has been centered around the following characteristics of the two methods of insuring: (1) service benefits of the associations, (2) the association nonprofit operation, (3) methods of rating, (4) advertising and promotion, (5) the servicing of national accounts, and (6) conversions and transfers. Each of these areas of difference will be examined below.

Service Benefits

The associations for years have emphasized that they provide coverage for specific "services" as opposed to the private carrier practice of providing "indemnity" for medical expenses up to stated dollar limits. Many Blue Cross plans do provide for full service on a variety of miscellaneous hospital charges, while private carriers usually provide some kind of stated limit in dollars for such services.

The difference between the two approaches in this respect is not as great as it might appear, however. Many association plans provide specific dollar limits for such items as X-ray examinations, and the majority limit daily room benefits to either semiprivate accommodations or a stated dollar amount. Association plans will also limit the number of days of room benefit coverage, as will private carrier plans. For expenses other than for hospitalization, the two approaches are quite similar in that they customarily use a benefit schedule with specific amounts listed for specific procedures or services. Only where the local medical society has agreed to accept the scheduled benefit as full payment can such a plan be considered full service. Most such agreements apply only to individual claimants with incomes below a stated level.

Another side of the service approach involves direct payment by the plan to the hospital or the doctor; and this feature has had a strong appeal to employees because of the ease of admission to hospitals without a cash deposit, and because of automatic crediting of benefits against total charges upon discharge. Private insurers have attempted to overcome this problem by working out admission agreements with hospitals, in which the hospital grants immediate recognition of insurance benefits by accepting a benefit assignment in lieu of a cash deposit and full cash settlement of final charges. The Health Insurance Council has led in the development of these plans.[6] Even without a formal admission plan, hospitals in recent years have become more and more willing to accept assignment of insurance benefits when they are convinced of the insurer's integrity.

The origin of medical expense reimbursement insurance throws some light on its subsequent development. Such insurance was originally designed to protect the accounts receivable of hospitals by a prepayment budgeting system,[7] and was not even intended as a system of insurance protection against large losses for the individual recipients of medical care. Even though protection of individuals may have been quite unintentional, it is difficult to see how these prepayment plans fail to be insurance. The associations have continued to expand the prepayment system, and it was perhaps logical that private insurers would offer similar competitive plans.

A second reason for continuation of first-dollar emphasis in coverage is the greater interest of both employers and union

---

[6] See Chapter VI for a discussion of these plans.

[7] See C. N. Walker, *Transactions of the Society of Actuaries,* Vol. 6 (1954), pp. 586–87.

leaders in employee goodwill than in sound insurance. This leads to providing benefits payable to the greatest number of people without regard to inadequacy of these benefits in a few instances.[8]

Private carriers began moving toward the major medical approach about 1950, but the association plans in general made no such move until ten years later. Their emphasis has continued to be on covering the high frequency losses; but the rising costs of medical care, along with the competition by private carriers, have moved them in the direction of expanded benefits, deductibles, and the use of the coinsurance feature at the upper levels of their benefit structures.

Association Nonprofit Operation

Most of the associations are chartered under special laws as nonprofit organizations; and since they pay virtually no taxes, this feature has given them a significant cost advantage over private carriers. They have also no doubt gained considerably in goodwill for this same reason, because they are able to attain a position of community sponsorship in their operations. The only way private carriers can overcome this disadvantage is to reduce expenses of other types below those of the associations.

Methods of Rating

Private carriers have from the beginning varied rates for group health insurance according to the experience of the individual group, or at least the large groups. The association plans have tended to follow what is usually called a "community" rating system where rates are uniform for the same benefits throughout the area of the association's operation. This has tended to lead to a loss of the larger and better groups to private carriers. To offset this, many association plans now place groups in different classes based on the experience of the individual groups, although they have not gone into experience rating to the extent the private carriers have.

---

[8] *Ibid.*

Advertising and Promotion

Much of the association advertising and promotional material has emphasized that there is no limit to the amount of benefit for most hospital services, other than room and board. This approach has a very strong appeal to employees, since they frequently have little or no opportunity to become acquainted with the details of either Blue Cross or private carrier plans.

A few companies have offered schedule benefits for hospital services without limit for some benefits under the schedule. Companies not using schedules point to available higher limits for miscellaneous services and attempt to show the economic soundness of the major medical approach to coverage.

Servicing of National Accounts

Since eighty-three separate and independent Blue Cross Associations were in operation in 1959, the associations traditionally have been unable to provide coverage for employers operating throughout the United States. To overcome this problem Blue Cross formed a stock company, Health Service, Inc., in 1949 to provide national coverage for large employers. Operating with its companion Blue Shield national organization, Medical Indemnity of America, Inc., the associations are able to compete with private carriers for national accounts.

Private carriers have enjoyed some competitive advantage by combining group health and group life insurance in a single package, with lower total administrative cost to the employer. This advantage may disappear, because the associations can enter the life insurance business simply by acquiring a life insurance company where state laws permit.

Conversions and Transfers

Blue Cross and Blue Shield have for years permitted employees under group contracts to change to an individual contract upon termination of employment in an employee class eligible for insurance. Private insurers did not start to offer the conversion privilege on any significant scale until about 1951, and conversions were few until private insurers began concerted efforts to extend coverage to retired individuals.

There are three reasons why an employee may wish to convert his medical reimbursement insurance to an individual basis: (1) he may desire to continue this coverage for himself and family when he retires, (2) he may wish to convert because he or one of his dependents is in poor health, and (3) he may desire to continue coverage until he becomes eligible for group insurance with a new employer.

The problems and practices of conversions and continued coverage after retirement will be examined in detail in Chapter XII. Conversions made because of poor health, of course, represent serious adverse selection; and such policies must be adequately rated on the individual basis, or a group must be surcharged for such conversions. The need for temporary protection in the interim between coverage under group plans has accounted for a large portion of all group health conversions and also for a large portion of the high lapse rate of converted coverage.[9]

Blue Cross and Blue Shield plans generally provide continuous coverage for employees moving from one group or locality to another through the Inter-Plan Transfer Program. Such a solution would be more complicated for private insurers because of the large number of such insurers, but the need for this type of conversion could be reduced by the more direct and inexpensive method of waiving a probationary period on new employees who have evidence of terminating group insurance.

Share of the Market

Table 4 shows the share of the total market for expense reimbursement insurance which private companies and Blue Cross–Blue Shield held from 1952 through 1959.

Private companies had a fairly substantial increase in the

---

[9] See Alan M. Thaler, A. Howard Hotson, and C. S. Lembkey, "Conversions —A & H," *Proceedings, Bureau-Conference Group Accident and Health Insurance Meeting,* 1955, pp. 63, 68.

TABLE 4

PROPORTION OF INSURED PERSONS COVERED BY INSURANCE
COMPANIES AND BLUE CROSS–BLUE SHIELD PLANS

End of Year	Hospital Expense		Surgical Expense		Basic Medical Expense	
	Insurance Companies	Blue Cross Blue Shield	Insurance Companies	Blue Cross Blue Shield	Insurance Companies	Blue Cross Blue Shield
1959	57.0%	43.0%	59.7%	40.3%	47.1%	52.9%
1958	56.5	43.5	59.8	40.2	47.5	52.5
1957	56.1	43.9	59.8	40.2	47.4	52.6
1956	55.5	44.5	59.7	40.3	46.7	53.3
1955	54.0	46.0	59.4	40.6	46.3	53.7
1954	53.8	46.2	60.4	39.6	46.1	53.9
1953	53.3	46.7	61.9	38.1	46.3	53.7
1952	51.9	48.1	62.1	37.9	44.2	55.8

Source: Life Insurance Association of America, *Group Insurance and Group Annuity Manual*, Vol. I, July, 1960, "Tables," p. 5.

hospital expense line, a modest increase in basic medical expense, and a modest decline in surgical expense.

COMPETITION AMONG PRIVATE INSURERS

The competition among private insurers is centered almost entirely on benefit scales offered, initial or ultimate insurance costs, or a combination of the two. Some emphasis is placed on service provided for groups, but this perhaps has less appeal than the others.

Benefits

Benefit plans are fairly standard for the basic group covers so competition on benefits usually takes the form of "frills" or fringe benefits. The addition of a new form of benefit with a strong appeal, such as a medical care allowance for accident only, results in a temporary advantage to the company originating the cover. If the cover has a good sales appeal, other companies soon follow suit in self-defense. If the hazard is considered insurable, a new benefit added by one company soon becomes a standard part of the package of all.

Costs

Competition on the basis of cost of insurance is a much more complex process. Claim costs should be approximately the same under identical benefit plans regardless of company, so emphasis is placed on "retention"—the portion of the premium to be retained by the insurer for expenses, contingencies, and profits. If this retention figure takes the form of a guaranteed maximum, the balance of the premium must be returned to the policyholder in the form of loss payments or a retroactive rate reduction.[10] Regardless of how much is needed out of a year's premium for expenses, loss sharing with other groups, and contingencies, the company has available only what is left after the guaranteed return has been made to the policyholder. Table 5 presents an example of a ten-year cost pro-

TABLE 5

TEN-YEAR COST PROJECTION OR RETENTION ILLUSTRATION
FOR GROUP HEALTH INSURANCE

Item	Disposition of First-Year Premiums		Disposition of Renewal-Year Premiums	
	Per Cent	Amount	Per Cent	Amount
Incurred claims	70.00	$26,046.72	70.00	$26,046.72
Retention charges:				
Commissions	11.70	4,360.00	1.75	651.17
Taxes	1.80	669.77	1.80	669.77
General administrative expense	12.00	4,465.15	7.00	2,604.67
Contingency reserves	1.80	669.77	1.80	669.77
Total retention	27.30	$10,164.69	12.35	$ 4,595.38
Dividend	2.70	998.19	17.65	6,567.50
Total of claims, retention and dividend	100.00	$37,209.60	100.00	$37,209.60

jection or retention illustration for a 300-life case with income reimbursement, hospital, and surgical expense insurance for employees, and hospital and surgical expense insurance for

---

[10] See Chapter VIII for a discussion of the retention in retroactive rate reductions.

dependents. The volume discount (see Chapter VIII) has been applied to arrive at the annual premium shown, and commissions are calculated from the usual commission scale shown previously in Table 3.

The retention illustration in Table 5 is realistic, but there are of course many variations that such illustrations might take for this same group. Some of the variations are based on legitimate differences between companies, while others may be based on misinterpretation or misapplication of facts. It is reasonable to expect that all companies will not incur the same expenses in handling even identical groups, so there might be variation in either direction from the 12 per cent and 7 per cent expense charges shown in the table. Other companies amortize larger parts of first-year expenses and commissions over several years, so some items might be shifted from first-year to renewal-year retention. The life company level commission scale would reduce first-year commission costs but increase the costs for renewal years.

Many variations in retention illustrations are the result of making the best possible use of available statistics. Some companies, instead of using illustrations particular to the circumstances of the case may use *average* expense rates for first and renewal years for all insurance the company has in force. Expense rates vary considerably between small and large groups, and average rates would not be applicable to a particular group except by coincidence. A company with a large premium volume in bigger groups would naturally have a relatively low average expense rate.

Occasionally an insurer will base retention illustrations on average figures or typical figures for groups of the same size. Then all of the groups comprising the average figures may not be administered the same as the group to whom the bid is submitted. Most presentations are of course honest and would not involve deliberate misuse of figures. However, groups having the same annual premium will still not necessarily have the same expense rates because of differences in turnover, industry, rate, and benefit levels.

In general, retention illustrations may mean less to the prospective policyholder than might be indicated by the preceding discussion. Even if a maximum retention is guaranteed, it is illustrated as a percentage of premium; and if premiums are increased in a renewal year, the *amount* of company retention can increase even though the *percentage* remains the same. It is not the practice to raise renewal premiums just to give the insurer a greater amount of retention, since competition would prevent it even if some companies wanted to raise premiums. However, rates are raised when a group shows consistently poor underwriting results, and a retention guarantee stated as a percentage of nonguaranteed annual premiums is to some extent suspect as a guarantee.

Retention illustrations or guarantees below 10 per cent of premium after the first year are not at all uncommon for the larger groups. Such low illustrations leave little margin for error within years before rates can be increased, and a margin is needed because expenses cannot always be controlled and contingencies are unknown. Because of the dangers involved in cutting the retention margin too low for safety, all retention agreements or guarantees are expressly prohibited for companies operating in New York.[11] For New York companies all retention illustrations or cost projections used in soliciting must be clearly labeled as such and not as guarantees. However, retention agreements are strongly implied in cost estimates, and companies not doing business in New York often make outright guarantees.

CHOICE OF COMPANY

Personal contacts play as great a part in placing group insurance as in any other line of insurance. Due to the emphasis on costs and the advent of insurance consultants, the importance of personal contacts may have diminished somewhat. Frequently an employer will have little choice of carrier when

---

[11] New York Insurance Department Ruling, December 21, 1949.

a union bargains for the insurance, and in such cases the influence of personal contacts may just be shifted rather than diminished.

The choice of carrier too frequently is made on the basis of inadequate cost projections, with resulting dissatisfaction when cost illustrations prove to have been too low. Because of the difficulty of changing companies later, the choice of carrier should be made on a sound basis. A change involves again undergoing the high first-year expenses and the possible loss of retroactive rate reduction credits.[12] The competition is, therefore, centered around new groups, because of the difficulty and expense of changing carriers.

A group should choose a company with full realization that each large group over a period must essentially pay its own way, except for possible catastrophes. The service provided a group by an insurer should be weighed carefully against the cost of that service. Finally, the choice should be made with full understanding of the close relationship between the contingency portion of retention and the stability of rates over long periods. Groups on a self-rating basis must pay their own losses and expenses over long periods, and retention of contingency funds during good years can reduce the chance of a rate increase after a poor year.

[12] Fred Slavick, The Operation of Sickness Benefit Plans in Collective Bargaining (Princeton University, Industrial Relations Section of the Department of Economics and Sociology Institute, 1951), p. 92.

CHAPTER VI

INSTALLATION AND ADMINISTRATION

THE successful and economical administration of a group insurance plan requires systematic procedures in a number of important areas. The installation of the plan might be considered merely a very important first step in administration, except that in a contributory plan a great deal of emphasis must be placed on selling the plan to the employees. Therefore, the material in this chapter will be discussed under the general headings of installation and administration.

INSTALLATION

The actual sale of the group insurance plan to an employer is followed immediately by all the necessary arrangements for putting the insurance plan into operation. In installing a group plan, it is essential that employer co-operation be secured before any active solicitation of individual employees begins.

A group plan is usually installed by salaried home office representatives after advance arrangements have been made for co-operation of executives and key personnel of the group policyholder. If the employer is to pay all the premiums, no solicitation of employees is necessary, but the employees must be informed of insurance benefits. However, the insurance plan must be sold to the employees if they are to contribute to premium payments. Insurance company representatives could conduct the canvassing of employees, but the canvassing is usually more effective when contact with the employees is handled by a representative of the employer.

Reports to the Company

When an employer requests an insurer to "bid" on a group contract, the agent, broker, or group representative submits the reports discussed below before a preliminary application is signed. On the basis of these reports the insurer will tentatively underwrite and rate the group and submit its bid. If the bid is accepted, the insurer's representative will then secure and send to the insurer the preliminary application and a deposit premium, for which a numbered conditional receipt is usually given the employer.

In many instances no bid will be involved, and the agent, broker, or group representative will send to the insurer the preliminary application, deposit premium, and all the other reports at the same time. The required reports and the preliminary application include details of the insurance plan and all the physical characteristics of the group in question. The timing of these reports is unimportant except in determining whether home office underwriting is done in two stages or one.

Proposed Insurance Plan. The preliminary application outlines the types of insurance selected by the group and includes a brief identifying description of the benefit plan selected for each type of insurance coverage. The form usually lists all the types of group insurance offered, and the types selected are merely checked to indicate group selection. Additional information may be entered in spaces provided for indicating applicable waiting periods, maximum periods of benefits, the inclusion or exclusion of maternity benefits, dependent coverage, and any other information necessary to describe the benefit plans.

Amounts of Insurance. The amounts of insurance to which each employee is entitled under all the different covers must be determined on some basis which will preclude individual selection against the insurance company. Accordingly, the preliminary application will contain a description of the method to be used in determining the amounts of insurance for individual employees and their dependents. The amounts of insurance are uniform for employees in any one classification, and the classes of employees are determined by factors or conditions related to employment. For a discussion of the methods used to determine employee classes, see Chapter II.

Eligibility Requirements. The preliminary application outlines the conditions under which new employees or new members of the organization may be added to the group or classes eligible for insurance. In the interest of stability and economical administration of the group, transient or temporary workers are effectively excluded from eligibility for group insurance by using a probationary period. The most common probationary period is three months, and new employees must serve out this probationary period before becoming eligible for the group insurance coverage. Requirement of a minimum number of work hours per week and that employees be actively at work serves to exclude from insurance coverage the part-time workers and those physically impaired when they might otherwise become eligible for insurance.

Previous Group Insurance Record. The record of previous group insurance may consist of a description of other types of insurance currently in force or it may describe any plans of insurance that have been in force earlier. The reasons for termination of current or previous insurance are considered important information for underwriting the group, and the previous insurance record may be necessary to determine commissions payable on the new insurance if issued to the proposed group.

Statements of Agent. The agent may be required to file with the preliminary application a detailed report concerning the group and the proposed method of administration. This report includes a record of branch offices, affiliates, and subsidiaries to be covered, with lists of the locations and numbers of employees in each location. This report may also contain detailed information concerning rate bases quoted and hospital admission plans in operation where the group is located.

Employees. The agent, broker, or group representative submits to the home office the total number of employees, with a breakdown showing the number eligible and not eligible for the group insurance. A further breakdown of the eligible employees gives the number of men and women and the number of older employees (over 60 or 65). Additional premiums are required when substantial amounts of the insurance are on female lives, and an additional premium may be required if the group contains a large proportion of older employees.

All these reports are evaluated in the underwriting process. If the group generally appears acceptable, preparation can be made for individual employee enrollment.

Announcements

Employees are furnished with an information folder or announcement outlining the benefits to be granted under the proposed group insurance plan. The distribution of this descriptive material is handled by the employer or under the employer's direct sponsorship, since this indicates to the employees that the employer has already given approval to the plan. A special effort is made to see that each employee is given a copy of the announcement material. Merely leaving the announcements in conspicuous places has proved ineffective in securing complete distribution of the material among the employees.

Conduct of Enrollment

Advance Preparation. A great deal of advance preparation may be necessary when a large group of employees is to be enrolled. Payroll deduction and premium remittance systems should be worked out in advance of the actual enrollment of employees, and most companies insist on a substantial advance payment from the employer. It is often considered desirable to enter each employee's name and department on an enrollment card in advance of the actual enrollment. Not only is this system efficient, but it personalizes the approach to each employee during enrollment.

Enrollment. A definite date is usually set for the enrollment, which is usually conducted during working hours. Attempts to enroll employees as they leave work or come to work have proved inefficient and ineffective in securing good participation.

Whether a plan is contributory or noncontributory, each employee to be insured must complete an enrollment card setting forth the information necessary for the issuance of the insurance. Of course, some employees may not wish to participate in a group insurance plan when they must contribute to premium payments. Companies usually secure from employees not electing the insurance a signed refusal card or a statement in which the employee waives his right to join the group insurance plan. There are several reasons for this practice: first, it provides an excellent check against overlooking some employees while canvassing for group insurance enrollment; second, it gives the employer and the insurance company written proof that the employee refused the insurance, if a question is raised later concerning a disability loss by the employee; and third, it requires the employee to take positive action as to whether he is or is not accepting the insurance, probably resulting in greater employee participation in the insurance plan.

Enrollment Cards

The individual employee's census card is necessary to supply the data upon which group underwriting can be based. Each card will supply the following information:

1. Name of the employee.
2. Date of birth.
3. Earnings classification.
4. Sex.
5. Occupation.
6. Date of employment.
7. Number and classes of dependents, if dependents are to be insured.
8. The types of insurance coverage offered.[1]

---

[1] Race of employees is not requested on present-day census cards, since requesting this information might be construed as racial discrimination. However, the agent reports to the company any unusual characteristics of the group which might indicate possible claims higher than normal. The enrollment card also shows the beneficiary, if life or accidental death insurance is involved.

When a group is to be contributory, it is necessary to secure a payroll deduction authorization from each employee to be insured. The payroll deduction authorization is usually a stub attached to the enrollment card. In addition to repeating the information necessary to identify the employee and the kinds of insurance selected, the authorization contains the employee's signature following a statement such as the one given below:

I hereby authorize my Employer until further notice, to take from my pay my contribution to the cost of Group Insurance for which I have made request and for which I am or may become insured as described in my Employer's current announcement, a copy of which I have received.

The census contains a list of the types of coverage offered, but each employee is not given freedom of election as to types of benefit. The employee is restricted to election of coverage for his dependents if such coverage is desired. The authorization portion of the card is retained by the employer as long as there is to be a payroll deduction for an individual employee's insurance. The authorization is usually signed without specifying the amount, because this eliminates the need to secure a new authorization each time rates or benefits change.

ADMINISTRATION

The administration of a group health plan involves handling all the details of collecting premiums, paying claims, and keeping records and certificates up to date. Administration begins as soon as installation is completed and continues as long as the insurance is in force.

The administration of a group plan requires detailed work in the following areas:

1. Issuing, replacing, and changing certificates.
2. Keeping records of insurance in force and changes in amounts of insurance.
3. Preparing monthly premium statements.
4. Enrolling new employees.
5. Settling claims.

All the procedures listed above comprise the administration system, except that the rather specialized work of settling claims is ordinarily considered a distinct administration process. Administration procedures may be carried on by the employer and the insurer jointly, or the employer may assume entirely the administration of the plan.

Insurer Administration

Administration by the insurer and employer jointly is commonly called "insurer administration" or "long-method" administration or accounting. This type of administration means that the principal functions of managing an insurance plan are carried out by the insurance company. The employer does little more than enroll new employees, report other changes in amounts and types of insurance, and remit premiums to the company when due. The insurance company handles all other details necessary to administer the plan.

When the home office underwriting indicates that a group is an acceptable insurance risk, the process of issuing the master policy and individual certificates begins. The insurance company prepares insurance register cards in duplicate for each insured employee within the group, and the home office keeps one set of cards and sends the duplicate set to the employer with the master contract. Individual insurance certificates are issued by the insurance company and are then sent to the employer along with the master contract and the register cards.

The employer is responsible for distributing the insurance certificates to the employees and recording all changes in amounts or types of insurance on the individual employee's register card. The employer reports to the insurance company all changes in insurance during each month. Separate reports may be filed for terminations or cancellations, additions to the group, reinstatements, addition of dependents, and changes in amounts of insurance due to changes in employee classification.

Whatever the mechanics of reporting, the insurance company must know the amounts of each type of insurance in force to prepare the monthly premium statement.

Group insurance premiums are payable in advance, and the monthly premium statement that the company sends to the employer is based upon the amounts of insurance in force at the beginning of the policy month. The figures for insurance in force are determined by adding all new insurance and increases in amounts of insurance to the amount of insurance in force at the beginning of the previous month, and subtracting all cancellations and decreases in insurance. To the extent that there are time lags between changes in amounts of insurance and their reflection in premium statements, the necessary premium adjustments are made in subsequent months.

Using the information submitted by the group policyholder, the insurer keeps register cards up to date, issues and revises certificates, and prepares the monthly premium statement to be sent to the policyholder. The principal methods of preparing monthly premium statements may be classified as either "manual" or "tabular."

Manual Administration. A manually prepared premium statement is divided into sections, with a section to apply to each form of insurance carried by the group. Insurance for dependents is treated in sections distinct from employee insurance, because different premium rates apply. Thus, for a group in which employees are covered by six forms of insurance (including group life insurance) and dependents are insured for three forms of insurance, the premium statement would consist of nine separate sections to determine the insurance in force for each of the nine insurance covers.

The amount of insurance in force at the beginning of the previous month is the starting point for determining this monthly premium due at the beginning of the current policy month. Additions to the group and increases in amounts of insurance must be added to the previous in-force figure to determine the maximum possible in-force for the current month. Additions to the group represent those employees (or dependents) who have become insured since the previous monthly premium payment was made. Reinstatements of lapsed insurance may be handled as new insurance, or may be brought into the total as an increase in the amount of insurance in force. Increases in the amounts of insurance, as evidenced by the employer's report of employee classification changes securing higher insurance benefits, mark the final additions to be made before deductions are made for reductions in the amounts of insurance.

Following the determination of the maximum possible amounts of insurance in force for the various covers, the employer is given credit for any insurance reductions for which no further premium payments are necessary. These insurance reductions may be in the form of reductions because of classification changes or because of insurance terminations. The total premium due is then determined by adding the premiums for each line of insurance. The premium for each line is the product of the applicable rate and the amount of insurance in force.

Some group contracts provide that a retroactive premium adjustment is made for partial months of coverage, usually with the assumption that additions and terminations occurred at mid-month. Other contracts provide that no retroactive adjustment will be made because it can be assumed that over a period the partial months of added and terminated insurance will cancel out. Because of its simplicity and economy of administration, the latter method is becoming more common.

Tabular Administration. The tabular method of administration entails the same insurer functions as the manual method, but the premium statement is prepared by tabulating machines. The insurer maintains insurance register cards for each employee in a group, and the information is transferred to punch cards. Using the punch cards, the tabulating machines prepare premium statements, showing for each named employee insurance in force by lines and any changes since the preceding premium statement. Some tabular systems begin the premium statement with previous totals of insurance in force and show only changes in insurance by named employees.

Whichever system is used, the employer can check changes and in-force figures on the statement with his own insurance register cards.

Self-Administration

The complete management of the group plan by the policyholder is called "self-administration," "self-accounting," or the "short method." Groups meeting the requirements of the insurance company may secure lower premium rates for group insurance by handling their own administrative details.

A fixed minimum number of employees is seldom required for eligibility for self-administration, and the minimum is varied according to the internal organization of the policyholder. A policyholder with centralized and efficient payroll and accounting systems may be eligible for self-administration with fewer than one hundred insured employees.[2] For groups with less desirable accounting methods, the minimum requirement for self-administration may be set at two hundred or more employees.

The policyholder assumes most of the duties that would be handled by the insurer under company administration. The policyholder keeps all insurance records, issues and revises certificates, and prepares the monthly premium statements.[3] The insurer will, of necessity, make use of its right to audit the policyholder's records, since there is no other method of checking to see that records are accurate and up to date. The insurer may make an audit at any time if the experience of a group is bad, but if a group plan appears to be operating smoothly, the company may make only occasional "spot-checks" rather than complete audits.

Claims Administration

The major function of a group insurance company is to pay all covered claims promptly and resist all false claims. The

---

[2] It is important that the payroll and accounting systems of smaller groups be centralized and efficient, because of the relatively greater expense of a necessary audit of a small group if records are decentralized or unsystematic.

[3] See page 120 for a discussion of self-administration of claims.

number of claims handled by an average group carrier is large although many of the claims are for relatively small amounts, so an efficient system of handling claims is necessary. A very important consideration in maintaining an efficient claim system is the simplicity of the claim form itself.

The Health and Accident Underwriters Conference has taken an active part in promoting standardized and simplified claim forms. Nonconference companies have developed their own simplified forms; but, in general, today claim forms are so similar and simple that employees and hospital attendants can easily supply the information requested by the insurer.

Much of the reluctance of hospitals and doctors in accepting commercial group insurance as an important source of compensation for services has been due to unwieldy claim forms and the lack of any guarantee that insurance benefits would be used to pay for services. The Health Insurance Council has been instrumental in developing simplified claim forms, direct payment of insurance benefits to doctors and hospitals, and hospital admission plans.[4]

Claim Forms.   Health insurance claim forms usually require that the employee, policyholder, and attending physician each fill in a section of the form. For medical care lines, the form will also include a section to be completed by the hospital, if hospital benefits are involved. The forms for the medical care lines of insurance also provide for assigning employee's benefits to the physician, surgeon, or hospital providing services.

The employee's section of the claim form requires the following information:

1. Identification, including name of the employee (and dependent if applicable), age, sex, and address.
2. Date of disability, if claim is made for income reimbursement benefits.
3. Time and location, if disability is due to accident.

---

[4] James R. Williams, "Hospital Admission Plans," *Group Proceedings, Health and Accident Underwriters Conference,* 1951, p. 24. See discussion below.

The employer supplies the following information on the claim form:

1. Identification, including the employee's name and the group and certificate numbers.
2. Amounts and types of benefits to which the claimant is entitled.
3. Dates when the employee left and returned to work.
4. Status of the claim under Workmen's Compensation coverage.
5. Any additional information that might be helpful in settling the claim.

The hospital supplies detailed information concerning:

1. Name and age of the claimant.
2. Time admitted and discharged.
3. Reason for hospitalization.
4. Nature of treatment.
5. An itemized listing of all charges made.

The listing of charges is necessary because hospital expense insurance benefits are divided into two separate categories. The company must know the nature of the charges to apply the allowance for extra charges only to those services not included in the room and board charge.

Physicians and surgeons are required to specify the nature of services rendered, when a claim is made for surgical or attendance benefits. Income reimbursement benefits are payable only when the claimant is under the care of a physician, and a physician's statement is required in connection with a claim for these benefits. This statement usually contains the following information:

1. Dates of treatments.
2. Diagnosis and nature of treatments.
3. Beginning date of disability.
4. Date the claimant was able, or is expected to be able, to return to work.
5. Explanation of any possible connection of the cause of disability with the claimant's occupation.

Assignment of Benefits.   Claim forms include the assignment form which, if executed, gives the company permission to pay benefits directly to the doctor or hospital providing services to the claimant. The form of the assignment is the same whether it is to a physician, surgeon, or hospital. A common assignment form is as follows:

I hereby authorize payment directly to (name of physician, surgeon, or hospital) of the (physician's attendance, surgical, or hospital expense) benefits otherwise payable to me, but not to exceed my indebtedness for charges made. (Date and signature)

The assignment gives the hospital or doctor a guarantee that any insurance benefits available will be used to pay for services rendered. The advantages of this system to doctors and hospitals is obvious, and the system benefits the claimant by relieving him of an obligation to pay his bills from his own pocket or wait for his insurance benefit. Payments to hospitals and doctors are limited to the amounts which the claimant owes for services, as the assignment is not intended as a "blank check" on full insurance benefits if benefits exceed the charges. If a claimant has a cash hospital expense benefit exceeding the actual hospital charge, the excess will be paid to the claimant.

Hospital Admission Plans.   Hospital admission plans give the group certificate holder immediate recognition of his insurance benefits. Without this recognition, the certificate holder usually will be required to make a cash deposit before entering the hospital and will be expected to pay his hospital bill upon discharge. Later reimbursement from insurance benefits does not remove the inconvenience and often the hardship accompanying a required cash outlay for services.

Hospital admission plans attempt to remove the necessity of the cash deposit by clearly identifying the benefits to which group certificate holders are entitled, and they provide a credit of these benefits toward the hospital bill. Of course, this credit can be granted only if provision is made for direct payment of the insurance benefits to the hospital.

There are two main types of hospital admission plans, commonly called the Index and Certification plans.[5] Under the

---

[5] For an excellent discussion, see Williams, *op. cit.,* pp. 24–25.

Index plan, group policies in an area are listed with a central council for hospitals, and this council relays the information to the hospitals. When a group certificate holder applies for admission, the hospital admission clerk confirms insurance coverage through the central council. The hospital then accepts an assignment of insurance benefits and the patient pays the difference, if any, between the insurance benefits and the total hospital bill.

Simplified and standard claim forms are used so hospitals can easily and quickly secure payment from insurance companies. The principal advantages of this type of plan are that the hospitals know immediately the benefits to which a patient is entitled, and the group policyholder and his employees need make no detailed arrangements before a certificate holder enters a hospital.

There is no central listing of group insurance policies under the Certification admission plan. The employer issues a certificate outlining the benefits to which the employee is entitled, and this certificate is presented at the hospital at the time of admission. Benefits are then assigned to the hospital, and the patient pays the excess charges, if any.

The principal disadvantage of the Certification plan is that a benefit certificate must be issued by the group policyholder for each hospital entry. The benefit certificate has a time limit (usually seven days) within which it must be used, otherwise a new certificate must be issued. Unless a time limit is set, former employees of group policyholders might attempt to obtain credit on expired insurance coverage.

Although employees must be educated to the procedures for using their insurance, the problems of detail are at least partly offset by uniform benefit certificates and elimination of registration with a central hospital agency. The principal advantages of the plan are its simplicity of installation and ease of administration by the hospitals.

These admission plans have resulted in much closer cooperation between insurers and hospitals and have served to reduce considerably the friction that formerly arose from a multiplicity of detailed claim forms and frequent failure of claimants to use insurance benefits to pay hospital bills. The ease of securing services through commercial insurance has enhanced considerably the value of commercial insurance to the insuring public.

Insurer Claims Administration. Claims administration by the insurer means that every claim from a group is submitted to the home office for handling. The insurer must, of course, maintain convenient and systematic records to process each claim.[6]

The first step in processing a claim involves checking the benefits and policy provisions for the group from which claim is made. A summary sheet for each group is maintained to show easily and quickly the amounts and types of benefits and covered losses. The nature of the claim and its cause are examined in light of the coverage provided by the master contract.

The second step involves determining the eligibility of the claimant for benefits on the basis of the pending claim. This includes checking to see that the insurance is in force and that the claimant is eligible to receive benefits.[7]

Once it has been established that the claimant is eligible for benefits, provision is made to pay the claimant the benefits to which he is entitled. Claims that involve continuous payments over a period are usually processed on a schedule that will permit payments to reach the policyholder at certain times. Terminal benefits are of course paid immediately, but income reimbursement benefits are usually timed to reach the policyholder at the end of each benefit week. The policyholder can then notify the insurer of terminations of disability, refund overpayments, or assist the claimant in submitting any necessary proofs of the continuation of disability.

---

[6] Claims administration by a branch office is essentially the same as home office administration, except that administrative functions are decentralized.

[7] Eligibility to receive benefits is especially important in settling claims of older employees if there is a maximum benefit period allowed each benefit year. It becomes important for all claimants where there is a question of extended insurance benefits or a restriction on claims due to the same or related causes.

Policyholder Claims Administration.   Policyholders may be permitted to administer their own claims, thereby effecting a reduction in the expense portion of group premiums. In general, only those groups eligible for self-accounting are permitted to administer their own claims.

The usual method of self-administration of claims is based on claim payments by drafts drawn by the policyholder on the insurer. The policyholder is given a draft book with the authority to pay claims with insurance company funds. The policyholder examines all claims, pays them if acceptable, and maintains all records of claims filed, refused, and paid. Copies of claim drafts are sent daily to the insurer, and these are the only claim records maintained by the insurer.

Since the policyholder maintains all claim records except copies of claim drafts, it is necessary that the insurer reserve (and exercise) the right to audit policyholder claim records.[8] The insurance company has a contractual obligation to pay any certificate holder all benefits for which he is eligible under the master contract, so care must be exercised that the policyholder does not refuse justifiable claims to effect a saving in premium. The contract must be followed to the letter in settling claims, because overpayment of claims could lead to serious losses to the insurer which might prove irrecoverable.

A few very large groups are permitted to administer their own claims by what is commonly called the reimbursement system. The policyholder pays all claims from his own funds and is reimbursed by the insurer, usually at the end of each month. In general, this system follows the same procedures as the draft book method, except that reports to the insurer are made monthly, either of closed claims or of total disbursements. There are two reasons why most companies do not favor the reimbursement system: first, companies in general prefer to use a check or a draft drawn on the company to show

---

[8] At least a partial audit is usually made each year, but complete audits are not made with any fixed regularity. Unusually high or low loss ratios may signal the necessity of an audit.

that it is directly discharging its contractual obligations; second, direct payments by the policyholder do not give the insurer the advantages of prestige and advertising commonly attributed to claim payments by the company.

Conservation

All contacts with policyholders are important in determining company-group relations. In a sense, then, all administration of group insurance is closely associated with the conservation of business. Poorly handled claims, or poorly answered questions or complaints, could easily lose a group to another carrier. Companies emphasize correspondence, assistance, and advice to policyholders.

Rates. Policyholders as a rule are extremely cost-conscious, so insurers must be able to give reasonable, simple, but factual reasons for rate levels and adjustments. This situation is magnified by competitive pressure, for other carriers are ready to submit proposals and cost estimates or projections when there is even a possibility that a large group is dissatisfied with its present carrier.

Answering cost and retention estimates of competing companies requires much painstaking work for a large group company. The result of this type of conservation is that each company attempts to outbid all others by using any available information to make its own cost picture appear superior to that of competing companies.[9]

Policyholders frequently ask the insurer to conduct a special claims study to determine why losses have been unusually high. These policyholders know that premium levels must be high enough to pay losses and expenses, regardless of which company provides insurance coverage. Claim studies are requested to isolate any correctible causes of high losses. Some common answers to high loss records are: low participation in the group plan, which increases adverse selection; un-

---

[9] See Chapter V for a detailed discussion of cost estimates or projections.

balanced benefit schedules, with poor spread of risk at the higher benefit levels; accident proneness or poor health conditions; malingering; and high frequency of maternity claims.

Participation.   The maintenance of a high level of participation in a group plan is a problem for both the insurer and the policyholder. Insurers suggest enrolling new employees at the time of hiring, because this is systematic and there is a psychological advantage to presenting the group insurance plan at the time application for work is made. When participation in a plan becomes low, companies usually assist the policyholder in staging an enrollment campaign. During these campaigns, eligible employees are usually enrolled without evidence of insurability.[10]

---

[10] See Chapter VIII for a discussion of medical waiver campaigns and the conditions under which they are conducted.

CHAPTER VII

PREMIUM RATES

THE total amount of monthly payment by a group policy-holder may be called the premium, but this amount is determined by applying the premium rates to the aggregate units of exposure for each of the group covers composing the total exposure of the group.[1] Under this system, group companies calculate premium rates separately for each unit of benefit provided by group health insurance.

There are several reasons for the individual "line" approach to premium rates. The lines of insurance were developed singly, and for each new type of benefit added, prediction had to be made of its cost. The multiplicity of benefit packages available has fostered a rating system that would charge each group a premium based on the nature and amounts of benefits provided. A stronger reason for the "line" approach is the constant company effort to find a reliable method of predicting the costs of any or all of the covers provided under group health insurance.

METHODS OF RATE CALCULATION

When an insurance cover is first written, there is no experience upon which to base a premium computation. The determination of a premium rate to be charged for the insurance must come before the experience, so rates during the

---

[1] See Chapter VIII for a discussion of rating and units of exposure. The charge per unit of benefit might be called a premium when viewed from the standpoint of the certificate holder, but it is a premium rate for the group policy-holder, regardless of whether the charge is per employee or per dollar of benefit.

original stages of any insurance are necessarily based upon judgment, assumptions, and any available statistical data that seem to parallel the expected experience. After a premium rate has been set initially, the rate maker may calculate new rates or modify old rates by either or both of two methods: the loss ratio method and the pure premium method.

Loss Ratio Method

The loss ratio method bases a revision or modification of the rate level upon a comparison of actual loss ratios to the expected loss ratios. Under this method, losses are not analyzed in relation to the units of exposure, but are simply compared with other losses. The approach is essentially from the standpoint of totals and not from the standpoint of experience of individual and possibly different units of exposure, and it provides "only a most indirect and uncertain guide for deciding whether a given individual risk belongs in this classification family or that."[2] Since the loss ratio method by itself provides no basis for classifying or reclassifying risks, "it is in fact not a method of *making* rates at all but a way of revising rates from time to time with an eye principally to an assurance of an adequate over-all rate level."[3]

Pure Premium Method

The pure premium method of making premium rates is not simply an adjustment of existing rates but represents a periodic reconstruction of rates, based upon an analysis of losses in relation to the unit of exposure. Unlike the loss ratio method, it can produce equitable rates between different risk classifications and at the same time provide over-all rate adequacy.

The first step in establishing manual premium rates is to derive pure premiums for a broad class of standard risks. The

---

[2] C. A. Kulp, "The Rate Making Process in Property and Casualty Insurance —Goals, Technics and Limits," *Law and Contemporary Problems, Regulation of Insurance,* School of Law, Duke University, Vol. 15, No. 4 (Autumn, 1950), p. 500.

[3] *Ibid.*

standard risk in all lines has generally been all-male exposure in the main bulk of standard industries, and subclassification of these standard risks has been effected in the loading process. This method requires collection of detailed statistics, not only for each line of group health insurance, but also for each type of benefit provided by a given line. The larger group companies collect such statistics from their own experience, and a wealth of statistical data has been supplied by the general and special studies of intercompany data supplied to a committee of the Society of Actuaries.

Once pure premiums have been calculated from appropriate statistical data, they must be "loaded," since pure premiums are for claim costs only and for standard risks. The loading, then, generally makes allowance for three additional items: (1) expense, (2) factors not accounted for in the basic pure premium, such as female coverage and effect of industry, and (3) a margin for contingencies.

Choice of Rate Making Method

The larger group companies generally use the pure premium method of calculating rates, although intercompany data usually must be modified.[4] Smaller companies usually use the pure premium method for income reimbursement and major medical rates, but they usually use a modified version of the loss ratio technique for rate calculation for the basic medical care covers. Intercompany data may have little application to the business in force for the smaller company, and analysis of its own experience is not only expensive, but the results might not be credible. Factors shown to affect claim costs, by the company's own experience and intercompany data, are given consideration in a rough judgment calculation of new rates. These new rates are then applied to the insurance in force in the company, and if they would have produced the desired underwriting results, the new rates are adopted for future use. Checking underwriting results, of course, includes

---

[4] See page 130 for a discussion of limitations of intercompany data.

a comparison of the new rates with the "going" rates for all lines.

The following discussion of rate calculation for the individual lines will deal only with the pure premium method, since this method applies to such a large portion of group insurance in force. The modified loss ratio method has been effective in calculating adequate rates (except for competitive pressure, which affects any rate-making method), but the problem of equity has been left to the retroactive rate adjustment formulas. Continuous refinement of methods of classifying and rating individual risks will lead more and more to use of a pure premium system.

ACCIDENT AND SICKNESS INCOME REIMBURSEMENT RATES

Original premium rates for income reimbursement insurance were necessarily based upon judgment, assumptions, and whatever statistical data were available. Cammack developed a premium rate table for income reimbursement insurance showing an annual premium applicable to insurance plans with different periods of indemnity, with a basic rate of $10 annual premium for $10 of weekly benefits for a period of twenty-six weeks, following a one-week waiting period.[5] This rate table, developed in 1918, was based on British experience of rates of sickness by age and duration, as shown by the Manchester Unity AHJ Table; and the table provided annual premium rates for standard industries and males only. Additional loading was required for women, industry, and for monthly premium payment.[6]

Following the publication of the Cammack table, there was no concerted action by the companies until the intercompany group morbidity investigation of 1931–35. Individual companies made their own rates, using whatever basis was at hand, with premium adjustments made by the loss ratio

---

[5] James D. Craig, "Group Health Insurance," *Proceedings, Casualty Actuarial and Statistical Society of America*, Vol. 7 (1920–21), p. 87.

[6] *Ibid.*, pp. 85, 89.

method. The only experience published for group income reimbursement policies during this period was that of two companies during the first half of the twenties.[7]

Many income reimbursement rate tables still in use today are based on the 1931–35 intercompany morbidity study. This study provided data for the construction of a premium table for income reimbursement insurance from which could be calculated premium rates for plans with any combination of maximum benefit and waiting periods.[8] This same study included special studies to determine the effect on premium rates of age, female coverage, industry, and size of group. Results showed that women developed claim costs approximately double that for men, the size of the group had little significance, claim costs varied widely by industry, and age distributions ordinarily did not affect claim costs if benefits to workers over age 60 were limited to a single maximum period of benefit per year.[9]

Pure Premiums from Intercompany Studies

The 1931–35 study provided a basis for calculating pure premiums, and a basic premium table was constructed which included a portion of loading.[10] In recognition of the possible need for more up-to-date data, a committee of the Actuarial Society of America began in 1947 an intercompany study of morbidity not only for income reimbursement, but for the basic medical care covers as well. The studies have been continued by a committee of the Society of Actuaries. These studies show annual claim cost per dollar of exposure for the six most common benefit plans, with costs broken down into ten groups according to the percentage of female exposure.

---

[7] Ralph Keffer, "Group Sickness and Accident Insurance," *Transactions of the Actuarial Society of America,* Vol. 28 (1927), pp. 5 ff. See also discussion by H. R. Bassford, pp. 264 ff.

[8] Gilbert W. Fitzhugh, "Recent Morbidity Upon Lives Insured Under Group Accident and Health Policies and Premiums Based Thereon," *Transactions of the Actuarial Society of America,* Vol. 38 (1937), pp. 357 ff.

[9] *Ibid.*

[10] *Ibid.*, p. 381.

There are several reasons why these claim costs are not directly suitable for pure premium calculation. In addition to the general limitations of intercompany studies to be discussed subsequently, specific limitations of results of these studies are evident upon inspection. Claim costs indicated do not show a consistent pattern for waiting periods, maximum benefit periods, or the effect of female exposure. A direct approach to claim costs would require analysis of both frequency and duration of disability.

A special study of the intercompany data was made in 1951. A disability continuation table was constructed, and from this was derived a basic male morbidity table (see Table 6) showing annual and monthly claim costs per dollar of benefit exposed for disabilities of given durations up to sixty weeks.

The basic morbidity table can be used directly for calculating pure premiums for benefit plans with any combination of waiting period and maximum duration in almost exactly the same manner the 1931–35 tables were used. However, the 1951 study was based on 1947–49 data, which represent very favorable morbidity years; and rates based directly on these data would include no margin for unfavorable experience, catastrophes, or the effects of an economic recession.[11] The indicated claim costs for the early days of disability are somewhat lower than might be expected if a first-day sickness plan should be written, because of adverse selection. For the same reason the difference in cost between plans with three- and seven-day waiting periods may be understated.[12]

For calculating pure premiums for plans with the same waiting period for both accident and sickness, use of the 1951 basic morbidity table involves two steps: to secure from the table the cost indicated for the maximum period of benefits plus the waiting period, and to subtract the tabular cost for the waiting period. The annual claim cost for one dollar of

---

[11] Morton D. Miller, "Group Weekly Indemnity Continuation Table Study," *Transactions of the Society of Actuaries,* Vol. 3 (1951), p. 54. See also discussion by C. E. Probst, p. 505.

[12] *Ibid.,* p. 54. See discussion by S. W. Gingery, p. 522.

TABLE 6

1947–49 Basic Morbidity Table for Males,
Group Accident and Sickness Insurance

Duration t		Tabular Cost per $1 of Weekly Benefit for Duration of Disability t or Less		Duration t		Tabular Cost per $1 of Weekly Benefit for Duration of Disability t or Less	
		Annual	Monthly			Annual	Monthly
1 day		0.0279	0.0023	17 weeks		0.7030	0.0586
2 days		0.0553	0.0046	18 "		0.7160	0.0597
3 "		0.0820	0.0068	19 "		0.7284	0.0607
4 "		0.1078	0.0090	20 "		0.7402	0.0617
5 "		0.1326	0.0110	21 "		0.7515	0.0626
6 "		0.1564	0.0130	22 "		0.7623	0.0635
7 "		0.1790	0.0149	23 "		0.7726	0.0644
8 "		0.1999	0.0167	24 "		0.7825	0.0652
9 "		0.2191	0.0183	25 "		0.7920	0.0660
10 "		0.2365	0.0197	26 "		0.8011	0.0668
11 "		0.2519	0.0210	26 ",	3 days	0.8049	0.0671
12 "		0.2659	0.0222	27 "		0.8099	0.0675
13 "		0.2788	0.0232	28 "		0.8184	0.0682
14 "		0.2908	0.0242	29 "		0.8266	0.0689
15 "		0.3021	0.0252	30 "		0.8345	0.0695
16 "		0.3129	0.0261	31 "		0.8422	0.0702
17 "		0.3233	0.0269	32 "		0.8496	0.0708
18 "		0.3333	0.0278	33 "		0.8568	0.0714
19 "		0.3430	0.0286	34 "		0.8638	0.0720
20 "		0.3524	0.0294	35 "		0.8706	0.0725
21 "		0.3615	0.0301	36 "		0.8772	0.0731
22 "		0.3703	0.0309	37 "		0.8836	0.0736
23 "		0.3788	0.0316	38 "		0.8899	0.0742
24 "		0.3870	0.0322	39 "		0.8960	0.0747
25 "		0.3949	0.0329	40 "		0.9020	0.0752
26 "		0.4025	0.0335	41 "		0.9078	0.0756
27 "		0.4099	0.0342	42 "		0.9135	0.0761
28 "		0.4171	0.0348	43 "		0.9191	0.0766
29 "		0.4241	0.0353	44 "		0.9246	0.0770
30 "		0.4309	0.0359	45 "		0.9300	0.0775
31 "		0.4375	0.0365	46 "		0.9352	0.0779
32 "		0.4439	0.0370	47 "		0.9403	0.0784
33 "		0.4501	0.0375	48 "		0.9453	0.0788
34 "		0.4561	0.0380	49 "		0.9502	0.0792
35 "		0.4619	0.0385	50 "		0.9550	0.0796
6 weeks		0.4977	0.0415	51 "		0.9598	0.0800
7 "		0.5265	0.0439	52 "		0.9645	0.0804
8 "		0.5505	0.0459	52 ",	3 days	0.9665	0.0805
9 "		0.5718	0.0476	53 "		0.9691	0.0808
10 "		0.5914	0.0493	54 "		0.9736	0.0811
11 "		0.6099	0.0508	55 "		0.9780	0.0815
12 "		0.6274	0.0523	56 "		0.9824	0.0819
13 "		0.6440	0.0537	57 "		0.9867	0.0822
13 ",	3 days	0.6508	0.0542	58 "		0.9909	0.0826
14 "		0.6598	0.0550	59 "		0.9950	0.0829
15 "		0.6749	0.0562	60 "		0.9991	0.0833
16 "		0.6893	0.0574				

Source: Morton D. Miller, "Group Weekly Indemnity Continuation Table," *Transactions of the Society of Actuaries*, Vol. III (1951), p. 55.

weekly benefit under a plan providing thirteen weeks of benefit following a waiting period of seven days would be determined as follows:

Tabular cost, 14 weeks	$0.6598
Less: tabular cost, 1 week	0.1790
Annual claim cost	$0.4808

For benefit plans providing a waiting period for sickness, but none for accident, separate calcuation is necessary. It was found in the 1951 study that the approximate division of costs between accident and sickness was one ninth for accident and eight ninths for sickness.[13] For a plan with thirteen weeks of benefit, a waiting period of seven days for sickness, and no waiting period for accident, the annual claim cost would be determined as follows:

Tabular cost, 14 weeks	$0.6598
Less: tabular cost, 1 week	0.1790
Annual claim cost	$0.4808
Tabular cost, 13 weeks	0.6440
$\frac{8}{9}(0.4808) + \frac{1}{9}(0.6440)$	$0.4989

Premium rates for plans with any combination of maximum period and waiting period can be calculated from the basic morbidity table in a similar manner.

Limitations of Intercompany Studies

It was mentioned previously that the 1951 morbidity table was based on data from a very favorable morbidity period, and there are other reasons why intercompany data must be used with care in calculating pure premiums. The figures are always out of date by two or three years by the time they can be compiled and analyzed; therefore, it is necessary to make allowance for any noticeable trends of claim costs.[14] Allowance must also be made for changes in economic conditions, personnel practices, geographical locations of groups insured, and the

---

[13] *Ibid.*, p. 56.

[14] See page 146 for a discussion of recent trends in claim costs in group health lines in general.

individual insurer's practices with respect to types of groups insured, claims administration, and underwriting requirements. Thus, many adjustments may have to be made before inter-company data can be used for rate making, and there seems to be no mathematical substitute for sound underwriting judgment.[15]

Loading Pure Premiums

It was pointed out previously that the loading portion of premiums must make allowance not only for expenses and contingencies, but also for the factors known to affect claim costs but not reflected in basic pure premiums.

Expenses and Contingencies. It is customary today to load pure premiums for expenses and contingencies in all group health lines to produce gross premiums applicable to all groups, and then to reduce the rates for larger groups by a scale of discounts based on premium volume. This system recognizes that all expenses and the margin for contingencies do not vary directly with premiums, and the scale of discounts increases with increases in total premium developed from all lines of insurance that are combined for commission and retroactive rate adjustment purposes.

It is impossible in a rating system to make allowance for all factors that might have a bearing on claim costs, so loading must include a margin to allow for these unknown or un-measurable factors as well as chance fluctuations from expected morbidity.[16]

The loading for each $10 of weekly indemnity suggested in the 1931–35 study was a constant of eighteen cents per month plus 15 per cent of net premium.[17] The same methods of loading and approximately the same amounts are in general use

---

[15] See discussion by H. J. Stark and W. W. Mincks, *Transactions, Society of Actuaries,* Vol. 4 (1952), pp. 155–56.

[16] See Edward M. Neumann, "Rates and Reserves—Group Contracts," *Accident and Sickness Insurance,* ed. David McCahan (Philadelphia: University of Pennsylvania Press, 1954), p. 211.

[17] Fitzhugh, *op. cit.,* p. 379.

today in loading pure premiums for smaller groups. Full manual rates so developed are first used in rating all risks, but the usual premium discount scale, shown in Table 7, is then

TABLE 7

RELATION OF MANUAL PREMIUM REDUCTION
FACTORS TO AGGREGATE MONTHLY GROUP
HEALTH MANUAL PREMIUMS

Initial Gross Monthly Premium	Percentage Reduction
Less than $1,000	0%
$ 1,000 and less than $ 1,250	1
1,250 " " " 1,500	2
1,500 " " " 1,750	3
1,750 " " " 2,000	4
2,000 " " " 2,500	5
2,500 " " " 3,000	6
3,000 " " " 3,500	7
3,500 " " " 4,000	8
4,000 " " " 5,000	9
5,000 " " " 7,500	10
7,500 " " " 10,000	11
10,000 " " " 15,000	12
15,000 " " " 20,000	13
20,000 " " " 25,000	14
25,000 and over	15

applied to determine final rates. The discount scale is a part of the filed rate structure of each group health company.

The percentage reduction indicated for a particular group is applied to the total gross manual premium for the initial month of the contract year. The percentage reduction is also applied to the manual rate, and this reduced manual rate is used to determine the total monthly premium for each of the remaining months in the contract year.

Female Coverage. Until a few years ago it was customary to charge double the male rate for female coverage if maternity benefits were included and an additional 50 per cent of the male rate if maternity coverage was excluded. Recent loading methods recognize that the two should be rated separately, because maternity benefits are independent of waiting periods and maximum periods for other disabilities.

The usual loading for female nonmaternity coverage is 65

per cent for thirteen-week plans and 40 per cent for twenty-six-week plans. A special investigation in 1949 indicated that the effective percentages of insurance on females for the female percentage groupings were about 6.5 per cent for the less than 11 per cent grouping, and the quinary points (15, 25, 35, and so forth) for the other percentage groups.[18] Most companies use an assumption of the quinary points throughout and calculate rates for the various percentage groupings by using a weighted average of the male and female rates. For example, under thirteen-week plans where the ratio of female to male costs is 1.65, the weighted average rate for the less than 11 per cent grouping is $0.95 + (0.05 \times 1.65)$, for the 11 to 21 per cent grouping it is $0.85 + (0.15 \times 1.65)$, and so forth. Similar calculations are made for twenty-six-week plans using a ratio of female to male costs of 1.40.

The premium rate for maternity benefits is calculated for all-female coverage, and then 5 per cent of this amount is added for the less than 11 per cent grouping, 15 per cent is added for the 11 to 21 per cent grouping, and so on. The maternity loading is a flat addition to each given percentage grouping for all benefit plans providing the same level of benefits, since the maternity cost is independent of waiting periods and benefit duration limits.

Industry. Extra loading for industry is required not only when occupational coverage is provided, but also may be required for nonoccupational coverage because of living conditions, general work conditions, or general quality of the labor force involved. Individual companies revise industry loadings occasionally as experience justifies revision, but a common scale of additional premiums required for nonoccupational coverage in a few industries is shown in Table 8. These same additional premiums are usually used for hospital expense and medical expense insurance also.

The increases in premiums shown in Table 8 are for a few principal industries only and represent minimum increases

---

[18] Society of Actuaries, *Report of the Committee on Group Mortality and Morbidity,* 1949, p. 26.

usually applied. A company may apply a higher increase to any group that appears to present unusual underwriting or industrial hazards.

Loading for occupational coverage is not uniform, but the loading may range from 5 per cent in the less hazardous

TABLE 8

INDUSTRY LOADINGS OF GROUP INCOME REIMBURSEMENT, HOSPITAL EXPENSE, AND MEDICAL EXPENSE INSURANCE PREMIUMS FOR CERTAIN INDUSTRIES

Industry	Percentage Increase
Distilleries of ethyl or methyl alcohol, or of alcoholic beverages	15%
Felt hat factories	*
Furriers	15
Lime, cement, gypsum (no quarrying)	15
Liquor and wine wholesalers	15
Marble and stone yards	15
Mines (surface and underground) and quarries	40
Railroads	25
Tanneries	15
Textile industries, by states	*
Woodsmen and loggers	25

* Individually rated.

industries, such as banks and insurance companies, to 75 per cent or more in industries such as mining and quarrying.

Age. Additional premiums are usually not required for insurance on older employees, unless the insurance on employees over age 60 is at least 10 per cent of total coverage. Both the 1931–35 and the 1951 morbidity studies indicated that claim costs begin to increase substantially beyond age 50, but these higher costs are absorbed in basic premiums unless the insurance on older employees is a greater proportion of total coverage than that of the average risk.

Some companies charge no additional premiums except for coverage on employees over age 65, but those over age 70 are usually assigned at least double weight in calculating the extra premium required. This system does make allowance for the very sharp increase in claim costs for those over age 65, but it requires absorption in the basic premium of the entire effect of age over the normal working span.

Assessment Reserves. The final items to be included in the loading of pure premiums are the amounts to cover the reserves for assessments for expenses and benefits to the disabled unemployed under state disability plans.[19] These additional loadings would of course not be required for rates for group health insurance plans generally.

Long-Term Income Reimbursement Rates

Although some of the principles discussed above are applicable, the tables and studies discussed in the preceding section are not appropriate for rate calculation for the more recently developed long-term income reimbursement insurance. There is no uniformity of rates for this type of coverage, since most companies are still experimenting with it. However, most companies base their rates on either their own experience with individual policies, with an adjustment for lower group administration costs, or on the Health and Accident Underwriters Conference modification of Class III disability rates.[20]

In general, an average one year renewable term premium rate is charged, and rates are affected by age, sex, and the size of the group.[21] However, some plans use an individual rate graded by age brackets and some use level rates graded by age of entry into the plan.

ACCIDENTAL DEATH AND DISMEMBERMENT

The problem of determining rates for accidental death and dismemberment insurance has not been as serious as that for other lines of group health insurance. This cover is almost universally considered by insurance men to be a "frill," offered

---

[19] See Chapter IX for a discussion of these reserves.

[20] Discussion by L. C. Cocheu, Jr., R. D. Albright, and H. F. Harrigan, *Transactions of the Society of Actuaries,* Vol. 10 (1958), pp. 745–48.

[21] *Ibid.*

only because its low cost offers a high and spectacular benefit when a claim does arise.

Pure Premiums

Pure premiums for this cover are based upon the chances that accidental death and dismemberment will occur within the interpretation of the rather narrow insuring clause, and the chances of fraudulent claim.[22] Current accidental death rates are presented annually from intercompany data studied by the group mortality and morbidity committee of the Society of Actuaries. Although these figures do not include data for dismemberments, these claims usually represent only about 6 per cent of total claims under this cover.[23]

Loading

Expense loading for accidental death and dismemberment insurance is very low in amount, since claim frequency is very low and general administrative expense is low, since this cover is rarely issued alone.

No female or age loadings are required for this cover, and the only loadings used are those for specific extra hazards (such as flying) and for industry, when occupational coverage is included. The annual studies by the committee of the Society of Actuaries provide a basis for occasional reclassification of industries. Industries are thus moved from one classification to another as experience indicates, but the rates for the five risk classes are similar for most group companies. Typical rates are shown in the following table:

Risk Class	Monthly Premium Rate per $1,000
Nonoccupational coverage	$0.06
Industry class, 24-hour coverage	
A	0.06
B	0.10
C	0.15
D	Individually rated

[22] John M. Laird, "Personal Accident and Health Insurance," *Transactions of the Actuarial Society of America,* Vol. 23 (1922), p. 381.

[23] Neumann, *op. cit.,* p. 210.

BASIC MEDICAL CARE

The problem of computing original premium rates for medical care covers was one of appraising the general costs of medical care, the nature of the benefits to be provided, and the possible effects on the costs of medical care that might be expected from providing insurance benefits. The results of a survey by the Committee on the Costs of Medical Care served as the starting point for calculating hospital expense insurance rates in 1934.[24] Rather general data and many assumptions served as the base for surgical insurance rates in 1938 and the other medical care covers as they were added during and after World War II.[25]

Pure Premiums

The intercompany morbidity studies begun in 1947 have included studies of claim costs for hospital and surgical expense insurance, with data classified into ten female percentage groupings. The combined 1947–53 policy years' experience was presented in the committee report for 1954 for the principal benefit plans.[26]

The intercompany hospital expense data are not considered generally suitable for rate making, because no distinction in cost is made between the room and board and extra expense charges. Since it was generally assumed that claim costs under hospital expense insurance varied directly with the daily room rate, the intercompany studies until 1952 show costs per dollar of daily room benefit. Most hospital expense plans today provide for reimbursement of extras up to a stated multiple of the daily room allowance, and recent studies indicate that the increase in cost under such a plan is less than in direct proportion to an increase in daily room allowance. For example, a $20 daily

[24] Gilbert W. Fitzhugh, "Group Hospitalization Benefits," *Record, American Institute of Actuaries,* Vol. 23 (1934), pp. 319 ff.

[25] See Wendell A. Milliman, "Insurance of the Expense of Medical Service," *Transactions of the Actuarial Society of America,* Vol. 41 (1940), pp. 126, 142.

[26] *Report of the Committee on Group Mortality and Morbidity, Society of Actuaries,* 1954, p. 94.

benefit costs less than double a $10 daily benefit, because the amount reimbursed by the insurer for hospital extras under the $20 plan will not be double that for the $10 plan.

The problem of rate calculation for hospital expense insurance differs from that for income reimbursement, in that continuation of disability or confinement is not the only determinant of cost. Claim costs for daily room service are a function of the confinement period, but this is not true for charges for additional hospital services, although these costs do vary to some extent with length of confinement. To meet the need for specific data concerning costs of the two benefits involved, a special analysis of intercompany data was made in 1952.[27]

This study produced basic claim cost and continuation tables for male employees, female employees, and the various dependent units, with maternity and nonmaternity costs segregated. The study also presented average charges for miscellaneous services under various amounts of insurance benefit, annual claim frequencies, and effects of age and geographical location on costs.[28]

From these data it is then possible to calculate the annual claim costs of the room and board benefit, the allowance for miscellaneous services, and the maternity benefit. These calculations are made separately for male employees, female employees, dependent spouses, and dependent children. The method of calculating the rate is the same for all the exposure units. The following is an example of this method applied to calculation of the annual claim cost for a male employee under a $10, thirty-one-day plan, with $100 miscellaneous charges allowance:[29]

---

[27] Stanley W. Gingery, "Special Investigation of Group Hospital Expense Insurance Experience," *Transactions of the Society of Actuaries,* Vol. 4 (1952), pp. 44–112.

[28] *Ibid.*

[29] *Ibid.,* p. 99, for claim frequency and annual daily benefit cost, and pp. 74, 76, and 81 for tables showing average miscellaneous charges. The $60 figure was used in the example for convenience, without reference to any particular geographical location.

Annual claim frequency   0.07
Average miscellaneous charge $60.00
Tabular cost, $1.00 of daily benefit $ 0.5656
0.07($60) + 10($0.5656) = $9.856, annual claim cost

Allowance for female coverage, maternity benefits, and other factors in construction of final rate tables will be discussed subsequently.

The calculation of surgical expense rates is a simpler procedure because only one type of benefit is involved. The intercompany studies show annual claim costs for each of the ten female percentage groupings, and these studies to date include costs under both the $150 and the newer $200 schedules. A special surgical claims study made in 1948 included an extensive analysis of both claim frequencies and surgeons' charges.[30] Using the special and the general studies, it is possible to calculate directly pure premium rates for all the various exposure units for both maternity and nonmaternity coverage.

A special surgical claim study in 1957 showed a substantial shift in both relative and absolute frequencies of many operations from those developed by earlier studies.[31] Such a shift indicates the need for periodic reappraisal of experience used in the calculation of surgical expense rates. In addition, it is likely that the relative value schedule developed from this study was influenced by the level and relative values of schedules in existence at the time of the study.[32]

Pure premiums for the various benefits provided by medical expense insurance have been calculated primarily from claim frequencies and durations derived from nonsurgical hospital confinement data and experience under the various plans. Rate calculation has been largely a matter of adjusting initial rates as they appear to be either inadequate or excessive. At present there is no solid statistical basis for these rates. Initial rates in

---

[30] Report of the Group Mortality and Morbidity Committee, "Group Surgical Claims Study," *Transactions of the Actuarial Society of America*, Vol. 49 (1948), pp. 142 ff.

[31] Morton D. Miller, "1957 Study of Group Surgical Expense Insurance Claims," *Transactions of the Society of Actuaries*, Vol. 10 (1958), pp. 359–487.

[32] See discussion by James B. Ross, *loc. cit.*, pp. 496–97.

general proved to be somewhat redundant, and reductions have been made in recent years on most of the plans.[33]

Following the calculation of rates for the different classes of dependents, these rates for all the basic medical care covers are then combined to correspond to different dependent units that will be encountered in rating a given risk. The rates are usually set up according to the following bases:

1. Single rate, which applies for one or more dependents.
2. Two-rate basis, which applies the first if there is only one dependent, and the second if there are two or more dependents.
3. Three-rate basis, which applies the first to a spouse only, the second to child or children only, and the third to spouse and child or children.

Loading

Loading basic medical care pure premiums for expenses and contingencies is essentially the same process as that discussed previously for income reimbursement. There is no loading of dependent medical care insurance rates for age, industry, or female coverage, but maternity and obstetrical benefits require a loading.

Employee covers require a loading for age and industry, and the loadings used are the same as those for income reimbursement insurance, except that no industry loading is required for surgical expense insurance. Maternity and obstetrical loadings are flat additions to each given percentage grouping for plans with the same maternity benefits; the amount of the loading varies only by female content of the group.

Loading for female coverage is handled by using a weighted average of male and female costs. The method is the same as that used for income reimbursement, but of course the ratio of female to male claim costs is not necessarily the same.

Recent studies and company experience indicate that geographical location has a marked effect on claim costs because of differences in availability of facilities, which affects utilization, costs of medical care, and the general attitude of em-

---

[33] Neumann, *op. cit.*, p. 220.

ployees, employers, and medical practitioners toward medical care and insurance. Rate systems are beginning to recognize these variations in manual rates.

MAJOR MEDICAL

The problem of calculating original rates for major medical was much more serious than that for basic coverage for a number of reasons. First, past figures did not reflect the large losses possible under the new type of benefit. It was also generally recognized that there would likely be a marked effect on costs by both age and income, neither of which had been considered important in basic plans. Second, the presence of insurance benefits in substantial amounts was almost certain to have a greater effect on claim costs than had been evident. Third, the potential liability under major medical was considerably greater than that under basic plans, and good judgment called for a great deal of caution in rate making. Fourth, it appeared that strong adverse selection would be inherent in an insurance plan which seemed to have appeal only to higher income employees and which could be sold in quantity only by completely re-educating the public away from bill-paying service to major coverage with both deductible and coinsurance features.

Pure Premiums

One of the earliest studies of costs of medical care for major medical rate calculation was conducted by Prudential among all its employees of assistant manager rank and higher.[34] The results of this study, although subject to a number of limitations to be discussed later, are still used as a basis for calculating pure premiums for major medical insurance, except where a few individual companies have developed and analyzed what they consider more acceptable data from their own plans.

This study analyzed claims under various deductible arrangements for employees, wives, and children; and it also

---

[34] See Alan M. Thaler, "Group Major Medical Expense Insurance," *Transactions of the Society of Actuaries*, Vol. 3 (1951), pp. 429 ff.

analyzed the effects of age, income, geographical location, and certain types of expenditures for medical care. The study showed that, contrary to the situation in other group health lines, age was an extremely important factor in determining claim costs. Table 9 shows the variations of claim costs for the different age groups under five deductibles.

TABLE 9

GRADUATED EMPLOYEE MONTHLY CLAIM COSTS FOR MAJOR
MEDICAL COVERAGE WITHOUT COINSURANCE, BY AGE GROUP

Age of Employee	Each Illness Deductible			Family Budget Deductible	
	$100	$300	$500	$300	$500
Under 35	$0.97	$0.47	$0.25	$0.58	$0.28
35 up to 40	1.27	0.60	0.31	0.69	0.34
40 up to 45	1.82	0.96	0.55	1.05	0.58
45 up to 50	2.40	1.34	0.81	1.50	0.91
50 up to 55	3.04	1.76	1.11	2.01	1.29
55 up to 60	3.77	2.24	1.47	2.60	1.76
60 up to 65	4.62	2.80	1.91	3.30	2.34
65 and over	5.62	3.46	2.45	4.14	3.05
All ages	2.25	1.25	0.77	1.44	0.89

Source: Alan M. Thaler, "Group Major Medical Expense Insurance," *Transactions of the Society of Actuaries*, Vol. 3 (1951), p. 448.

The study also showed that claim costs for dependent wives increase with higher employee ages, but not as rapidly as the employee claim costs, and that the rate of increase with age for males is relatively greater with the larger deductibles. Claim costs for dependent children decrease with higher employee age, because of a smaller number of dependent children.

Claim costs increase markedly with age because deductibles rule out many high-frequency but low-severity claims at young ages, while claims become more severe at older ages. Claim costs were found to increase considerably at high incomes, but for a different reason: persons in the higher income groups demand and are willing to pay part of the costs of the best medical care available.[35] Table 10 shows graduated claim

[35] Discussion by Alan M. Thaler, *Group Proceedings of the Health and Accident Underwriters Conference*, 1952, p. 58.

TABLE 10

CRUDE MONTHLY CLAIM COSTS FOR EMPLOYEE, WIFE,
AND CHILDREN FOR MAJOR MEDICAL COVERAGE
WITHOUT COINSURANCE, BY INCOME GROUP

Annual Income	Each Illness Deductible		
	$100	$300	$500
$ 4,000 up to $ 5,000	$ 4.58	$2.37	$1.51
5,000 up to 7,500	5.09	2.52	1.40
7,500 up to 10,000	6.00	3.20	1.93
10,000 up to 15,000	9.20	4.79	2.69
15,000 and over	12.48	8.68	6.72
All incomes	5.56	2.87	1.69

Source: Alan M. Thaler, "Group Major Medical Expense Insurance,"
Transactions of the Society of Actuaries, Vol. 3 (1951), p. 449.

costs from the study at different income levels for three deductibles.

Generally, income will tend to vary fairly closely with age. This was supported by special analysis of the data of the major medical study. Early rating systems for major medical generally assumed that rates graded by age would allow for the effect of income on claim costs, if there was a reasonable spread of incomes. However, most rate systems today, including Blue Cross and Blue Shield plans, provide for the grading up of rates for higher income groups.

The Prudential study also included an analysis of expenditures by type, and data from this analysis can be used directly for rate calculation where the major medical plan places specific limits on certain types of benefits, and where a major medical plan is designed for integration with a basic medical care plan. However, a number of other factors must be considered before such data can be used for pure premium calculation.

The application of a coinsurance requirement will not necessarily make a reduction in claim costs in proportion to the coinsurance percentage of medical care expenditures where major medical is not involved. Allowance must be made in rate calculation for the fact that the insurance will increase expenditures for medical care and that a coinsurance requirement has only limited effect in keeping costs down. The presence of insurance will generally have a greater effect on medical expenditures for persons in the lower income groups, but the coinsurance requirement is most effective in keeping costs "reasonable" in these same groups.

Modification of basic statistics is necessary to allow for the effect of different methods of applying maximum benefits and the deductible—such as, whether a deductible is applied only once to a given illness or whether it is applied more than once for expenditures over long periods. Allowance must be made for a single application of the deductible in case of common disaster, since a reduction in number of deductible applications will increase claim costs. Claim cost trends should be considered, since data are usually two or three years old by the time they can be compiled and analyzed.

In calculating rates for comprehensive coverage, some companies use their own base plan experience, add the cost of additional benefits, and give credit for the deductible and coinsurance features.[36] The additional costs and credits can be estimated from regular major medical experience.

Loading

Expenses and Contingencies.   Loading for expenses and contingencies is essentially the same process as that discussed previously for income reimbursement insurance, with two exceptions. First, claim settlement expenses are generally considered higher because major medical benefits may be paid at intervals over longer periods of time. Second, this type of insurance is still in the experimental stage, and many things about costs are unpredictable, which indicates that a higher margin for unfavorable experience is required.

Female Coverage.   There is considerably less effect on claim costs by female coverage than is found in the other health lines, primarily because the deductible excludes payment for

---

[36] For a discussion of this method of rating a group being changed from a base to a comprehensive plan, see W. S. Thomas, *Transactions of the Society of Actuaries,* Vol. 10 (1958), pp. 82–83.

many of the high-frequency but low-severity claims of females. The usual practice is to charge no additional premium where female coverage comprises less than 25 per cent of total coverage in a group.[37] There is at present no sound basis for determining the effect of female claim costs, but an arbitrary method of rating, where women comprise more than 25 per cent of a group, is to shift them into the next higher age bracket before calculating the average rate.

Geographical Location. Basic medical care covers are generally not loaded for geographical location, because benefits are kept at a reasonable level as part of the underwriting process. No such control is possible under major medical unless inside limits are placed on benefits for different types of expenditures. Most companies, therefore, vary their rates by geographical location for major medical.

EVALUATION OF RATE MAKING

Manual Rate Level

The wealth of data supplied by the various intercompany studies could provide a base for manual rates that would be adequate for losses, expenses, and contingencies, if companies make proper allowance for their own variations from intercompany averages. The many special studies make it possible to secure reasonable relativity between rates for risks placed in special subclasses, and retroactive premium adjustments can be made to allow for credible variations from class averages when these variations are not predictable in practice.

Competition has been the deterrent to calculating initial rates with generous safety margins. All important factors affecting costs can be considered in calculating rates, but the voice of an actuary falls on deaf ears when his rates would price the company out of the market. Formulas are, therefore, varied to make initial rates fall in general line with rates of other companies. Occasionally changes are made in rates for the various health

---

[37] See Neumann, *op. cit.,* p. 223.

lines, but eventually final rates are usually made by watching over-all loss ratios. And as long as acceptable total results are produced, there is no deviation from current rates. There has been a consistent upward trend in medical care costs since the intercompany studies were begun in 1947, and a downward trend of claim costs for income reimbursement insurance was reversed after a low in 1951.[38] Income reimbursement insurance showed a reduction in claim costs again in 1955 and 1956, but the trend turned upward again in 1957.

Table 11 shows the secular trend of claim costs for income

TABLE 11

SECULAR TREND OF STANDARDIZED MORBIDITY RATIOS FOR GROUP WEEKLY
INDEMNITY INSURANCE, HOSPITAL, AND SURGICAL EXPENSE
INSURANCE, 1952–58

Base: 1956–58 Policy Year's Experience

Year	Weekly Indemnity, All Plans, Nonrated Industries	Employees, All Industries		Dependents, All Industries	
		Hospital, All Plans	Surgical, All Plans	Hospital, All Plans	Surgical, All Plans
1952	101	87	91	93	94
1953	102	91	95	96	96
1954	102	93	96	95	97
1955	96	93	97	95	96
1956	99	98	98	97	99
1957	100	99	100	102	100
1958	100	105	102	101	101

Source: Society of Actuaries, "1959 Reports of Mortality and Morbidity Experience," *Transactions*, No. 2, 1960, p. 166.

reimbursement, hospital expense, and surgical expense insurance from 1952 through 1958, with the 1956–58 policy years' experience as the base.

Claim cost trends have not always been followed carefully in establishing general rate levels, but even if they are followed strictly, resulting rates will have a safety margin only if trends are projected. Rates generally cannot respond rapidly

---

[38] *Report of the Group Mortality and Morbidity Committee of the Society of Actuaries,* 1954, pp. 89, 94.

enough to prevent serious losses to some insurers even when total losses for all companies follow the general trend. In a serious upward shift in the trend, which could be caused by an economic recession, rates could not respond rapidly enough to forestall general losses.

Rate Equity

The emphasis in company rate making and in securing regulatory authority has been primarily on assuring an over-all initial rate level that would produce adequate premiums. But industry, age, and female loadings do represent attempts to secure equity among policyholders. Also, it is true that the retroactive rate adjustment formulas (to be discussed in detail in Chapter VIII) work toward equity.

Obviously the very large risks develop experience that is highly credible, and no individual small risk can ever be expected to pay its own way exactly. Placing large and small risks in different rate adjustment classes does permit small groups to benefit from generally favorable experience in their own class, but in this respect competition becomes a limiting factor.

Loading methods (discussed previously) set manual rates at a level to provide for expenses and contingencies for small groups, and then a volume discount is applied to recognize expense savings expected in insuring larger groups. Expenses definitely will be relatively lower for larger groups, but contributions for general contingencies should be related to exposure and not necessarily to premiums. Company experience and the intercompany studies indicate that the very large groups frequently develop claim costs relatively higher than those for small groups. If both large and small groups operated on the same premium base, a lower expense rate in large groups would leave a margin for higher loss ratios. The volume discount anticipates the expense saving and thus may leave a much smaller margin in premium to absorb higher claim costs for large groups unless the rating scheme makes other commensurate adjustment.

CHAPTER VIII

UNDERWRITING

UNDERWRITING group health insurance involves an analysis to determine if the group is to be accepted or declined for insurance under the proposed or a modified plan. A group is usually considered acceptable if it meets the legal and insurer requirements for type of group, minimum size, and minimum participation; and company underwriting rules are modified from time to time to fit changing conditions in the competitive picture. The decision to accept or reject a group is seldom based on hard and fast rules but on the application of these rules made flexible by variations in rates to be charged. Classifying and rating risks are therefore the most important phases of the entire underwriting process.

The underwriting process begins when a group first applies for insurance but does not end when the group becomes insured. The underwriting process must also be applied to groups wishing to renew a contract and to individual employees and dependents seeking to become insured under a group contract already in force. Accordingly, the underwriting process may be divided into three stages:

1. Initial underwriting, which is the selection and rating of new groups.
2. Renewal underwriting, which is the selection and rating of groups applying for renewal of an existing contract.
3. Individual selection of employees and dependents being added to a group, where individual selection is necessary.

The following discussion deals separately with these three stages of underwriting.

INITIAL UNDERWRITING

The process of initial underwriting involves an analysis of all the characteristics of a group which affect its general acceptability and the factors considered to have an effect on the cost of providing insurance to the group. If the group is considered acceptable after these characteristics have been analyzed, premium rates are then determined on the basis of the expected cost of providing the insurance, subject to the insurer's minimum rate level as filed with the state insurance departments.

Selection Factors

Benefit Plan. Benefit plans are carefully checked to insure a proper grading of insurance so there is a reasonable spread of risk at each benefit level. Care must be exercised to avoid overinsurance which might encourage malingering. Under-insurance must be avoided in hospital expense insurance, because an extremely low daily room rate usually leads to charges for additional services higher than anticipated in the rate. In addition, many underinsured employees feel dissatisfied and perhaps obliged to purchase individual policies, which means that group insurance for these has not been a solution to their problems.[1] The general company practice is to set hospital benefits approximately at the level of costs for semiprivate care and income reimbursement benefits at no more than two thirds of gross income.

Participation. Group insurance is based upon mass selection of lives, so requiring participation of a substantial percentage of eligible employees is the only method of combating adverse selection, since individual evidence of insurability is usually not required. Under many group laws, individual underwriting is permitted and companies may use this technique for the very small groups or the larger groups where there

---

[1] J. E. Hellgren, "Group Insurance—Its Problems and Outlook," *Proceedings, Bureau-Conference Group Accident and Health Insurance Meeting,* February 7–9, 1955, p. 6.

is a low percentage of participation. Participation requirements apply only to employees eligible for insurance, but any substantial difference between the total number of employees and those eligible for insurance must be considered with care to be sure adverse selection is not inherent in the group.

Eligibility Requirements. Eligibility requirements may be varied to suit any particular policyholder, but the insurer usually attempts to establish requirements that will exclude from coverage all temporary and part-time workers. Too short a requirement for the probationary period would lead to more selection against the insurer and a higher turnover within the insured group with a resulting higher cost of administration.

Previous Group Insurance Record. Any group applying for insurance to replace similar coverage with another carrier must be underwritten carefully and the reasons for changing carriers considered. It is common to require the group to submit the experience from the previous insurance plan, especially if the policyholder has originated the placement of the insurance with a new carrier. The most common reason for changing carriers is a threatened rate increase because of poor experience, and a new carrier should evaluate the experience to determine if it is correctable through change of plan or claims administration. Unless the reason for poor experience can be isolated and a plan for correction can be formulated, a transferred group may prove to be a very undesirable risk.

Size of Group. Before passage of the state disability laws, the major group companies frequently set minimum group requirements at twenty-five or fifty employees. In recent years there has been a shift toward writing group instead of franchise insurance for smaller groups. The original impetus for this shift no doubt came from the state disability laws. The shift has continued because of an increasing company recognition that properly underwritten small groups can produce acceptable underwriting results. One reason for this is that individual small groups are not in a position to apply as much pressure for lower rates as the large groups.

There are, however, a number of problems connected with the underwriting of small groups. Most of these are due to high expense ratios, the greater possibility of selection against the company, and the difficulty of administration.

A part of the problem of high expense ratios stems from the fact that in the smaller groups the insurer is sometimes dealing with employers with poor accounting procedures, and this in turn may lead to difficulty in servicing the groups. Employment with the smaller employers may be less stable than with the larger groups, and it may be impossible to continue to meet minimum participation requirements. A high rate of termination in the early policy years is costly because of the higher first-year expenses including first-year commissions to agents. In addition, many expenses, such as premium billing and dividend calculation, are relatively fixed regardless of group size. Some of these problems may be solved by having the agents install and service the small groups and by paying them a service commission continuing for the lifetime of the group.[2]

Many companies today require individual evidence of insurability in the smaller groups, particularly those with fewer than ten employees. Many require 100 per cent participation, or at least greater participation than the usual 75 per cent minimum requirement for groups with twenty-five or more lives. If these participation requirements are not met, evidence of insurability is often used for individual underwriting.

In smaller groups there could be considerable selection against the insurer through choice of benefit plan. Most companies today attempt to insure small groups with standardized benefit plans, so sales and service may be handled by ordinary agents instead of group specialists and to reduce the possibility of adverse selection through benefit plans. This procedure is sound in purpose, but even small employers may want several benefit plans from which to choose. Experience indicates that plan simplification frequently must give way to competitive

[2] K. M. Briegel, "Cases of Less Than 25 Lives," *Group Proceedings Health and Accident Underwriters Conference,* 1950, p. 62.

necessity; some companies offer a variety of plans to small groups.[3]

Type of Group. As pointed out in Chapter V, companies are willing to insure any type of group permitted (or not prohibited) by law, if effective underwriting rules can be devised. Underwriting of most groups is based on the factors already discussed, but there are a number of additional underwriting problems connected with insuring labor negotiated plans.

Since the Inland Steel case and Cross case decisions holding insurance to be a proper subject for collective bargaining, insurance has become a principal demand in labor contract negotiations second only to wage increases.[4] As a result of this increased interest in insurance as a bargaining subject, the joint employer-union trust has become the most common type of trusteed plan.

An insurer is in a poor position to make even a preliminary quotation on rates and benefits unless the trustee for an employer-union trust has already established the administration machinery and secured preliminary census data on employees to be covered. If this has been done, the principal questions over which difficulties may arise in bargaining for group insurance are amounts and types of benefits, who pays the costs of the insurance, and benefit eligibility requirements.

The question as to amounts and types of benefits is, of course, directly related to the question of who is to pay the costs of the group insurance. The demand for the most complete protection available must be measured against willingness to pay for such protection, and unions argue that money to pay group insurance premiums is actually wages earned by employees.[5] The extent to which the employer is willing to pay the costs

---

[3] Frederick T. Googins, "Group Coverages on Less Than Twenty-five Lives," an address presented at the Educational Seminar, Bureau of Accident and Health Underwriters, February 2 and 3, 1954.

[4] P. G. Korn, "Collective Bargaining in the Group Picture," *Group Proceedings Health and Accident Underwriters Conference*, 1950, p. 45.

[5] *Ibid.*

of the protection desired by the union becomes a major point to be resolved in negotiations. As a corollary, the choice of insurance carrier becomes important, because union negotiators are usually interested in the lowest possible rate quotations to secure the maximum benefits for the money available.

Many problems of administering negotiated plans may arise unless the insurer can require that both initial and continuing eligibility for coverage of a union member be based on a contribution on his behalf to the premuim fund, otherwise the trustee may at some time not have the necessary funds for premiums. Initial contributions to the premium fund usually must be based on hours worked before the insurance becomes effective, and continuing contributions usually must be based on a minimum number of work hours. Both these definitions of eligibility in terms of hours worked are essential because most employer contributions to such funds are based on a cents-per-hour formula.[6]

Rating

The rating portion of the initial underwriting process involves determining the first-year premium rates to be applied to each benefit unit of the group. The benefit units, or units of exposure, for the group health covers may be stated as follows:

1. Each $1.00 (or $10) of weekly indemnity for income reimbursement.
2. Each $1,000 of principal sum for accidental death and dismemberment.
3. Each employee, dependent, or dependent unit at each level of daily rate for hospital expense insurance.
4. Each employee, dependent, or dependent unit for each surgical schedule.
5. Each employee, dependent, or dependent unit for the various types of medical expense insurance.

---

[6] For an excellent discussion on trusteed plans, see Edwin P. Brooks, Frederick T. Googins, and A. R. Willson, addresses at Educational Seminar, Bureau of Accident and Health Underwriters, *Eastern Underwriter,* January 30, 1953, pp. 33–34.

Once the manual premium rates for the units of exposure have been determined, the calculation of the premium for a group is a process of applying the manual rates to the total units of exposure.

Some of the rating factors are allowed for in the rate tables, but some require separate calculation since they are not applied frequently enough to warrant inclusion in the tables. The tables allow for the effects of female coverage, maternity and obstetrical benefits, and separate costs of hospital room benefits and extra services. Separate calculation is required for industry loadings, unusual underwriting hazards, and volume discount.

An example of rating an individual group is given in Table 12. The group to be rated has the following characteristics:

1. 300 insured employees, with 5 per cent female coverage.
2. 200 insured dependent units, multiple rate basis (wife and children).
3. Class A industry, nonoccupational coverage.
4. Income reimbursement insurance, with benefits first day for accident, eighth day for sickness, twenty-six-week maximum benefit period, no maternity benefits.
    a) 120 Class 1 employees, $50 weekly benefit.
    b) 180 Class 2 employees, $40 weekly benefit.
5. Hospital expense insurance, employees and dependents, thirty-one-day reimbursement plan, $10 daily benefit, $200 limit for extras, $100 maternity benefit for dependents only.
6. Surgical expense insurance, employees and dependents, $225 schedule, obstetrical benefits for dependents.
7. Accidental death and dismemberment.
    a) 120 Class 1 employees, $3,000.
    b) 180 Class 2 employees, $2,000.

Any additional premium required because of industry or unusual hazards would have been applied to the rates before they were used in the calculations in Table 12. Once the total manual premium is determined from full manual rates, the premium volume discount is applied to determine the actual premium for the first month. The risk used in the example will receive a volume discount of 7 per cent (see Table 7, page 132), and the initial monthly premium will be $3,133.91.

TABLE 12

EXAMPLE OF RATING A GROUP HEALTH RISK

Coverage	Rate Unit	Rate	Number of Rate Units	Total Premium
a) Employees				
Accidental Death:				
Class 1	$1,000	$0.060	360	$ 21.60
Class 2	1,000	0.060	360	21.60
Accident and Sickness:				
Class 1	$1.00	0.088	6,000	528.00
Class 2	1.00	0.088	7,200	633.60
Hospital Expense	Employee	1.560	300	468.00
Surgical Expense	Employee	0.590	300	177.00
b) Dependents				
Hospital Expense	Employee	4.750	200	950.00
Surgical Expense	Employee	2.850	200	570.00
c) Total Manual Premium				$3,369.80

RENEWAL UNDERWRITING

The renewal underwriting process ordinarily begins two or three months before the anniversary date of a group contract. Renewal underwriting differs in one respect from initial underwriting, in that the insurer usually does not have the right under the contract to refuse to renew the contract unless participation in the insurance plan is below the minimum number or percentage required. However, premium rates are guaranteed for only one year, so the insurer could induce the employer to cancel by a substantial increase in premium rates.

Renewal underwriting, then, is centered primarily around the problem of determining the premium rates to be quoted for the coming year, and the related problem of determining any retroactive adjustments to be made on the current year's premium. To solve these problems, the insurer usually considers claims and expenses for both current and past policy years, and the underwriter must evaluate this experience in light of its probable significance.[7] Both retroactive and prospec-

---

[7] Experience of only nine or ten months of the current year is available, because data must be assembled and evaluated in time to have renewal rates ready by renewal date. Many group carriers handle all rerating and retroactive adjustments at the end of each calendar year. This makes the full contract year's experience available for the latest contract year.

tive rate adjustments will be based to some extent on past experience of a group, but companies usually try to avoid a sharp increase in premiums at the end of the first policy year. There are two reasons for this: first, experience for a single year may not be a sufficiently reliable basis for an increased rate level; second, expenses are always high the first year and "clean-up" claims may account for high first-year losses.

Retroactive Premium Adjustments

Group health contracts may be either participating or nonparticipating, just as in other lines of insurance. Policy-holders are eligible for dividends on each policy anniversary, if the contract is participating. If the contract is nonparticipating, there is no direct sharing in underwriting profits by the policyholder. However, nonparticipating contracts issued today provide that, although there are no "dividends" in the usual sense, the company may make adjustments in premiums, and any adjustment may be made retroactive for one year.[8] Although there is a technical difference between the two in reporting premiums, the result is essentially the same to the policyholder: a set premium for one year with the possibility of a refund at the end of the policy year.

There are two basic approaches to the problem of making retroactive premium adjustments: the tabular method and the asset share method.[9] The first is applied to the smaller groups where the credibility of experience is low and expense rates are usually high. The second is applied to the larger groups where the credibility of experience is higher.

The tabular method usually consists of a set of tables showing the refund percentages of premium, which vary by such

---

[8] The New York law provides that premium adjustments may be made retroactive for one year only, and that the amounts so paid may be used to reduce the employer's contributions to premiums, but that any excess over the employer's contributions is to be applied to the benefit of the employees. See Art. 9-A, Sec. 221, par. 9.

[9] Edward M. Neumann, "Rates and Reserves—Group Contracts," *Accident and Sickness Insurance,* ed. David McCahan (Philadelphia: University of Pennsylvania Press, 1954), p. 207.

factors as amount of premium, claim rate, and policy duration. The total amount to be returned to groups falling under this system is apportioned without detailed and expensive studies of actual claims and expenses for each group.

The amount of redundancy in premiums charged larger groups may be relatively less than that in premiums charged smaller groups, but a very large group with a good loss record may have a substantial amount of premium redundancy. Competition is a strong factor in giving weight to an elaborate premium refund formula for larger groups, because these groups demand specific consideration of their own claims and expenses if experience has been good. The following discussion deals with formulas used to calculate retroactive premium adjustments for groups under the asset share method.

Retroactive Adjustment Formulas

Retroactive adjustment formulas are usually determined once or twice annually, unless a change at some other time appears necessary.[10] The formulas vary by company, and in the same company the formulas or the factors considered vary over a period of years. However, the principles involved and the factors considered are essentially the same, even though their relative importance may differ.

In any rate adjustment formula the group is given credit for earned premiums. In some instances credit is also given for interest earnings on advance premiums and special contingency funds. Any retroactive premium refund is determined by subtracting all charges against the group from the total credit of earned premiums and investment earnings.

Losses. For groups whose experience is given full credibility (see later discussion of credibility), each group will be charged with the losses that have been incurred during the policy year,

---

[10] The formulas are not made a part of group contracts issued by most companies, because these companies feel that variation of the formulas is the most effective way to adjust total refunds to the amount of surplus available for distribution. However, some casualty companies use retrospective rating, where rate adjustment factors are included in the group insurance contract.

while for groups with less than full credibility, each group will be charged with losses falling somewhere between actual and expected losses.

Expenses. Expenses to be charged to a group are calculated as accurately as possible and practicable. Although more elaborate methods of expense allocation are used by some companies, the usual practice is to charge each group with three expense items: (1) a flat charge per contract, (2) a flat charge per life insured, and (3) a percentage of premiums. The more elaborate systems use detailed cost accounting to charge each group with commissions, taxes, actual costs of handling, and an acquisition charge for the first year. Whatever system of allocation is used, the heavy first-year expenses usually cannot be charged off completely the first year but must be amortized over several years, with allowance for losses from interest and lapses.[11]

Assessments. Assessment charges for state compulsory disability plans, if applicable, are charged to the group. The actual or estimated assessment charges are allocated to each group on the basis of covered payroll of the group in relation to the covered payroll of all groups.

Contribution to Contingency Reserves. An important item to be charged against each group is the portion of the premium to be retained by the company for possible over-all unfavorable experience in the future. This contribution is charged through the rate adjustment formula.

Credibility in Adjustment Formulas

The credibility of a group's experience refers to the weight that can be given to the actual morbidity experience of the group. In general, the weight given to the experience of an individual group will vary with the number of lives insured and the length of time the contract has been in force, and, in some formulas, by claim frequency and duration. A large group would be expected to develop more credible experience than a

---

[11] Neumann, *op. cit.,* p. 209.

small one, and experience of a group over a period of several years should be more reliable than the experience of a single year. As the exposure measured in life-years of a risk increases, the individual experience becomes more credible until on the very large and older groups the experience may approach (but not necessarily reach) 100 per cent credibility.

The credibility "factor" in rate adjustment formulas is concerned primarily with current and issue-to-date life-years of exposure. The credibility factor may be subdivided (in some formulas) into two factors: one to be applied to current-year experience and the other to be applied to total experience from date of issue of the contract. Although the total effect depends upon the weight given to the two subdivided factors, the separate application of the two makes it possible to assign any desired weight to current-year experience.

The use of two factors also makes it possible to recognize that past experience may have little bearing on current experience, if there has been considerable turnover within the group over a period. Losses developed by one group of employees many years ago will actually have no bearing on losses developed by current employees, except that in many groups the same employment practices would tend to keep the same class of employees in a given group. The application of a single factor assumes for its accuracy a fairly static group and tends to minimize the effects of unusual experience in current years the longer the contract stays in force. The use of a single factor would tend to make rates more stable over time, but the use of two factors is probably justified in that rates can be made more responsive to changes in morbidity rates, whether the change is caused by group turnover or some other factor.

Most rate adjustment formulas recognize one additional element in determining the credibility of the experience of a group. Experience becomes more dependable with a larger number of group covers, because of the broader base for losses and the packaging approach to rating. If some lines show losses, others may provide a margin to carry the group without a loss on the entire package. This makes a smaller over-all retention possible and increases the possibility (or the amount) of a retroactive premium reduction.

Premium Adjustments

It was pointed out previously that the total charges against a group are subtracted from the total credits of the group. If a positive balance remains to an individual group, this represents the amount of the retroactive premium adjustment. If a negative balance remains, the group has been carried at a loss for the year and no adjustment is possible. However, when credibility is relatively low, the application of a formula may produce a positive balance even though the group has actually been carried at a loss. The application of a retroactive rate adjustment formula is demonstrated below, both for losses below the expected and above the expected. This demonstration assumes a case with one hundred lives, $10,000 annual earned premium, $7,000 of expected losses, and $2,200 of incurred expenses (including the contribution to contingency reserve). The dividend formula is:[12]

DIVIDEND = EARNED PREMIUM − (CLAIMS CHARGED + EXPENSES), with claims charged $= zA + (1 - z)E,$ where:

z = Credibility factor (assume 0.6 for this case).
A = Actual losses.
E = Expected losses.

1. Assuming actual losses of $6,500, the claims charged will be:
$0.6(6,500) + 0.4(7,000) = \$6,700.$
The dividend is: $10,000 − ($6,700 + $2,200) = $1,100.
2. Assuming actual losses of $8,100 (greater than expected), the claims charged will be:
$0.6(8,100) + 0.4(7,000) = \$7,660.$
The dividend is: $10,000 − (7,660 + 2,200) = $140.

It can be seen from the examples above that losses charged to the group will fall between actual and expected, with the actual point determined by the credibility factor. It can also be

---

[12] The formula given is for illustrative purposes only, and was suggested by a group actuary as one which would demonstrate the relationship of the various factors in the formula. Actual formulas used currently are company secrets.

seen from example 2 that with relatively low credibility a group can receive a dividend although it has actually been carried at a loss—$300 in the case shown.

The figures used in the above dividend illustration were for one year only and some dividend formulas deal only with current-year experience. The usual practice, however, is to apply such formulas on a cumulative basis from date of issue. The formula would be used in exactly the same way, with these exceptions:

1. Actual losses, expenses, expected losses, and earned premiums would be cumulative since issue of the contract.
2. The credibility factor would be slightly larger in each succeeding year.
3. Current dividend would be determined by subtracting total previous dividends from the current cumulative formula answer.

Prospective Rate Adjustments

Insurance companies allow deviations from manual rates in advance when it appears that the experience of a group calls for a deviation. Rate increases are usually avoided at the end of the first policy year, unless underwriting results have been very poor, but thereafter rates may be increased to whatever level appears necessary to make the group pay its own way. Because the policyholder might change companies, no attempt is usually made to force a group to make up for past losses out of premium increases, but the group may not be eligible for any dividends or retroactive adjustments until all past losses are repaid. This last applies only to moderate losses, since major losses are simply spread over all groups and no recovery is attempted.

Essentially the same factors used in retroactive premium adjustments are used to consider prospective rate changes. If a group showed a 10 per cent loss in the current policy year, there is good reason to believe the premium for the coming year should be increased to cover a possible loss of the same amount. Conversely, if a group received a retroactive refund for the current year, there is some justification for granting an advance reduction of the coming year's premium in anticipation of a similar record.

Advance rate reductions by formula are usually limited to groups of fairly large size (such as five hundred) or groups with a large number of life-years exposure. Ordinarily, no advance reduction will be made unless the experience of the group has been consistently good for the period since issue. Advance reductions are nothing more than anticipation of retroactive refunds, so the retroactive-refund history is an important guide to the wisdom of allowing advance reductions.

The amount of an advance reduction of premium ordinarily will be limited to the usual retroactive refund, but greater reductions may be allowed on a "reserve" basis. The policyholder establishes with the company a reserve equal to the amount of the excess of the reduction over the usual retroactive refund. This, of course, gives no additional reduction the first year, but the advantage to the policyholder is that the reserve must be paid only once, if future experience is good. Once the reserve becomes impaired, this portion of an advance rate reduction will no longer be allowed unless the reserve is replaced.

UNDERWRITING ADDITIONS TO GROUPS

There is no underwriting problem in adding new members to a group if the plan is noncontributory, since new members are added automatically when they become eligible for the insurance. New members of contributory groups must choose whether to become insured or remain outside the insurance plan.

Additions without Individual Selection

It is not necessary that the company underwrite individually all additions to a group insurance plan. It is to be expected that there will be turnover within the group, so new members of the group are permitted to join the insurance plan without underwriting, if election of the insurance is made within a reasonable time. The principle followed in this respect is that adverse selection will not be serious if new members of the group are added no later than thirty-one days after they become eligible. This system is used in most group insurance plans. New members of a group are allowed complete freedom of applying for insurance any time during their probationary periods or within thirty-one days thereafter.

Additions with Individual Selection

When new members of a group have failed to elect the insurance during the time when they could do so without evidence of insurability, their subsequent election of the insurance calls for individual underwriting to guard against selection against the company. Individual underwriting is also considered essential for employees requesting insurance cancellation while actively at work and later desiring to enroll again for insurance.

The company must try to avoid insuring those applying for insurance because of recently discovered or changed conditions of health.

Individual underwriting of employees and dependents is based upon evidence of insurability submitted to the insurance company. The evidence usually takes the form of a statement from the employee or dependent regarding health with collateral statements from the employer concerning the apparent general condition of the applicant's health, performance of full duties, and any irregularity of attendance at work, with reasons for the irregularity. The health statements of the employee provide the insurance company with information in five general areas:

1. The general health of the applicant.
2. Any recent absences from work due to sickness or injury.
3. Medical treatment or consultation during the past year.
4. Contemplation of hospital treatment or surgical operation.
5. For female applicants, pregnancy existing at the time application for insurance is made.[13]

---

[13] Existing pregnancies are usually excluded from the coverage of late applicants, even if the group plan provides immediate maternity benefits for others.

The information submitted by the employee in these five general areas is in much less detail than that for nonmedical applications for health insurance on an individual basis. However, the information secured for underwriting group insurance outlines in general the present health of the applicant, his recent medical history, and any anticipated future medical treatment. The insurance company, in all events, reserves the right to require a medical examination if the information contained in the employee's or employer's statements indicates that the applicant might be uninsurable. Although some insurers pay the cost of a required medical examination, most plans provide that the employee must submit evidence of insurability at his own expense.

To obtain accurate information in the employee's statement of health, the company requires a supporting statement from the employer and a signed statement from the employee that the information submitted by him is true and correct. Such a statement from the employee may take the following form:

It is understood and agreed that the foregoing statements and answers are correct and wholly true, and that they are the basis on which insurance may be issued under the group policy. Furthermore, it is understood and agreed that the Company reserves the right to request that, at my own expense (or the Company's expense), I be examined by an accredited Medical Examiner selected by the Company. (Signed)

Statements submitted by the employer are merely supplementary to those submitted by the employee. No employer's statement is required when the applicant for insurance is a dependent. The employee enrolling for minor dependents is required to supply the information and to sign the application for insurance.

Medical Waiver Campaigns

When it becomes apparent that new employees are not participating in a group insurance plan to the extent desired, the insurance company may conduct a "medical waiver" enrollment campaign. During such a campaign, employees who would otherwise be required to submit satisfactory evidence of insurability are allowed to enroll for insurance without such evidence. Since the applicants are not individually underwritten, it is necessary to conduct the campaign only under certain controlled conditions.

The length of time for the campaign is usually limited to not more than two weeks. In addition, a common practice is to require that none of the insurance becomes effective unless at least 50 per cent of those eligible but not insured at the beginning of the campaign apply for insurance during the campaign. A minimum number of new enrollments may be set, such as ten, otherwise none of the insurance on newly enrolled employees becomes effective.

CHAPTER IX

RESERVES

RESERVES for group health insurance are essentially the same as for any other line of casualty insurance: they are actual or potential liabilities of the insurance company. These liabilities may be divided into insurance, business, and contingency reserves, but since business reserves are not peculiar to insurance, this chapter will deal only with the insurance and contingency reserves for group health insurance.

A group company must calculate its year-end reserve liabilities for inclusion in the annual statement; it must also calculate contract-year reserves to determine amounts to be charged to each policyholder in retroactive rate adjustment formulas.[1] The principles involved in both calculations are the same; in fact, identical factors may be used in both, but contract-year reserves are generally given more detailed analysis.

RESERVES FOR ANNUAL STATEMENTS

Unearned Premium Reserve

The unearned premium reserve represents the aggregate amount of liability of the insurance company in carrying all policies to their expiration dates. This liability is composed of three parts: (1) premiums paid in advance, (2) earned retroactive rate refunds, and (3) the unexpired portion of current gross premiums in force.

Premiums paid in advance are completely unearned, so the

---

[1] Edward M. Neumann, "Rates and Reserves—Group Contracts," *Accident and Sickness Insurance,* ed. David McCahan (Philadelphia: University of Pennsylvania Press, 1954), p. 202.

total amount of these is included in reserve. The amount of reserve for retroactive rate refunds is the amount of refund ac-
crued from the last anniversary date to the date of reserve
valuation, as determined by the retroactive refund formula applicable to each group. This reserve may include prospective
rate refunds projected to the next policy anniversary.[2]

Most of the unearned premium reserve is made up of the
unearned portions of gross premiums in force on the date of
valuation. The unearned portion of any premium is that proportion of the total premium that the unexpired period bears
to the full period for which premiums have been paid.

Since an unearned premium reserve is necessary to carry
policies to expiration dates, it is quite properly required by law
in all states. The New York insurance law makes the following
provision concerning the unearned premium reserve:

> Every insurer authorized to transact business in this state shall
> (except for life and related contracts) maintain reserves equal to the
> unearned portions of the gross premiums charged on unexpired or
> unterminated risks and policies.[3]

The premium base upon which the reserve is to be computed
is not pure but gross premium. The company is not required
to reserve on the basis of all premiums received during the
year, but only upon those actually in force at the time of reserve
valuation, since no unearned premium reserve would be needed
for completely earned premiums.

If the requirement that reserves be maintained "equal to the
unearned portions of the gross premiums charged" were carried out to the letter, it would mean that the insurer would be
required to determine the unearned premium separately for
each policy in force. Companies with a volume of business too
small to warrant the expense of modern statistical machines
would find it economically impossible to make such calculations. Accordingly, the law generally provides that a less accurate but more practical method may be used to compute the
reserve.

---

[2] *Ibid.,* p. 203.

[3] Art. 5, Sec. 74, par. 1.

The method usually prescribed for one-year policies is the fifty-per-cent method, which means that an unearned premium reserve must be established equal to one half the gross premiums in force at the time of valuation. This method assumes that annual premium policies are written at a uniform rate throughout the year and that the average policy was written at the middle of the year, with six months of its term still unexpired on December 31. For monthly premium policies the assumption is that the average premium due date was December 15, or that the due dates were spread uniformly through December. These assumptions are not necessarily correct; if the volume of business grows during the period, the unearned premium reserve will be too low, and if volume declines, the unearned premium reserve will be too high.

Another assumption inherent in calculating the unearned premium reserve on a gross premium base is that expenses are paid uniformly as the policy moves toward its expiration date. This assumption is incorrect, because expenses are heaviest at the beginning of the period for which premiums are paid and this works always in the direction of reserves higher than necessary.

In periods of a growing volume of business, the two basic assumptions underlying the fifty-per-cent method tend to produce errors in the opposite direction. In periods of a declining volume of business, both assumptions make for reserves higher than the true reserves should be.

That policies may not be written uniformly throughout the period is a possibility in any line of casualty insurance, but perhaps peculiar to group insurance is a marked regularity in the deviation from uniformity. The majority of group premiums are paid shortly after the beginning and middle of each month, because premium remittances are most conveniently handled by the employer in conjunction with the handling of his payroll. These two peak periods of premium payments within each calendar month produce the same effect on the size of the unearned premium reserve as would be produced by a generally declining volume of business. In recognition of this concentration of premium payments, most large group companies compute the unearned premium reserve on a daily pro-rata basis, even though it is somewhat expensive to do so.

This method consists of determining the total unearned premium reserve by adding the unexpired portions of all premiums in force. The unexpired portion of a given premium is obtained by multiplying the gross premium by the fractional part of the total premium period unexpired. This is done by punch cards simultaneously for all policies having the same expiration date and same period for which premiums have been paid. To illustrate, monthly premiums paid through January 1 will be $\frac{1}{31}$ unearned on December 31, since there is one day of the premium period unexpired of the original total of thirty-one days.

Premiums on expired policies are merely dropped from the record, and on the date of valuation the premium cards for premiums still in force are sorted and tabulated by expiration date. The unearned premium reserve can then be determined by applying the appropriate factors ($\frac{1}{31}$, $\frac{2}{32}$, and so on) to the premiums in force for each expiration date.[4]

The unearned premium reserve calculated by the pro-rata method will usually be lower than the reserve calculated by the fifty-per-cent method, since the concentration of premium payments early in each month has the same effect on the required reserve as a sharp decline in premium volume. Using accurate methods to produce lower unearned premium reserves has little to do with company solvency. The unearned premium reserve is relatively unimportant compared with premiums written because of the preponderance of monthly premium payments. In view of this relationship, the requirement of an unearned premium reserve does little to safeguard company solvency without the coexistence of an adequate rate structure.

---

[4] To avoid the peak load at annual statement times, companies frequently make their unearned premium reserve studies as early as June or July. These studies establish the relationship between gross premiums in force and the unearned premium reserve, and this relationship is used for reserve calculation at the end of the year, unless there has been a substantial shift of expiration dates for insurance in force.

Loss Reserves

While the unearned premium reserve represents company liability expected to arise after the date of reserve valuation, it makes no provision for obligations incurred but unpaid before the valuation date. These obligations include unsettled claims and the expense of settling the claims. Unsettled claims include not only those approved but unpaid and those in process of settlement, but those incurred but not yet reported.

Since both the known and unknown claims may be incurred in one period and discharged in some later period, it is necessary to require a claim or loss reserve to liquidate these unsettled claims. The New York insurance law makes the following provision for claim reserves:

> . . . every insurer shall maintain reserves in an amount estimated in the aggregate to provide for the payment of all losses or claims incurred on or prior to the date of statement, whether reported or unreported, which are unpaid as of such date and for which such insurer may be liable, and also reserves in an amount estimated to provide for the expenses of adjustment or settlement of such claims.[5]

The claim reserve proper does not include all the expense of adjusting and settling claims, and a separate reserve is established for unallocated claim expenses. The method of computing loss reserves is not prescribed by law, but reserves are estimates of amounts required for payment of all losses, reported or unreported, if the losses are unpaid as of the date of reserve valuation. There are two generally used approaches to loss reserve calculation—one involves separate calculation of known losses and incurred but unreported losses; the second involves calculation of the two together.[6]

Known Loss Reserve. The aggregate known loss reserve for all the health covers combined is determined by multiplying the number of outstanding claims of all kinds by an aver-

---

[5] Art. 5, Sec. 72.

[6] This discussion will deal with separate calculation of the two. When the calculation is combined, exactly the same principles and practices are followed as those discussed later for calculating the reserve for incurred and unreported losses.

age value per claim.[7] The average value is determined from the company's past experience on closed claims by dividing the number of known claims into the total amount of the claims less the amounts which had been paid before valuation date. For example, a company finding from past experience that the average unpaid value of all reported claims (including those approved but unpaid and those in course of settlement) is $85, would then multiply this figure by the total number of current year's known claims of all kinds. The result would be taken as the aggregate reserve for known losses.

Using an average value requires careful judgment by those computing the reserves, since average values developed in the past would not be applicable to current claims unless the same general conditions existed. Judgment of these conditions may be based on the general trend of average values developed over a period or may be based on a more direct consideration of the factors which might make an average value from past experience inapplicable to current claims.

An average value per claim may have been perfectly stable over a long period, but a sudden shift from a full employment economy to widespread unemployment and lower wages would certainly require that good judgment set reserves higher than would be indicated by average values developed during the high employment period. Consideration must also be given to any general changes in the costs of medical care or the availability of facilities for providing medical care, since the latter affects claim duration. One of the most important factors to be considered is the ratio of income reimbursement and major medical coverage to the total business in force in the company. Offhand estimates by group actuaries indicate that the known-loss reserve for income reimbursement will usually be 7 or 8 per cent of annual premiums for this cover and perhaps

---

[7] The reserve for accidental death and dismemberment insurance is usually calculated separately by an individual inventory of each claim, since the claim frequency is relatively low and liability of the company is usually definite. Reserves for long-term income reimbursement insurance are calculated by the tabular method, using either a claim continuance or disabled life annuity table.

10 per cent for major medical, while the known-loss reserve for basic medical care covers will be only 1 or 2 per cent of annual premiums for these covers. Thus any increase in the ratio of income reimbursement or major medical to total in force will obviously require an increase in the average claim cost used in computing known-loss reserves.

Reserve for Incurred and Unreported Losses. Determining reserves is somewhat different for incurred and unreported claims. Even though the reserves themselves may not be determined immediately at the end of a year, there is no definite time limit within which a company could assume that all claims had been reported that were incurred during the period before the reserve valuation date. An average value cannot be assigned to unreported claims because their number is not known, unless the number can be derived. The unknown-loss reserve is therefore usually calculated as a percentage (based on past experience) of some convenient current base.

One common way of ascertaining the incurred and unreported reserve is to determine the ratio between claims that were incurred and unreported at the end of a given year to the claims paid during the last quarter of that same year. This ratio is then applied to claim payments made during the last quarter of the current year to determine the current-year reserve.

The ratio to be used cannot be calculated until claims have had time to mature, and ratios for three or more years are usually used to avoid chance fluctuations and to allow for any trend. An example of such ratios for three years is shown in Table 13, with an application of an indicated ratio used for reserve calculation in the fourth year.

The actual ratios in the table for the three years for which the study is complete show a slight upward trend; therefore, the ratio of 0.4200 is a reasonable assumption for reserve calculation at the end of 1960. This ratio multiplied by the amount of cash claims for the last quarter of 1960 gives an incurred and unreported loss reserve of $1,008,210.00. Any convenient base for a ratio could be used, such as premiums, losses paid during a twelve-month period, losses paid in one month only, or claims incurred during a given period. Premiums may not provide a good base, because such a ratio would assume a fixed relationship between premiums and losses which may not exist. Losses during a period of twelve months may be unresponsive to changes in claim reporting trends, and losses for one month are subject to considerable chance fluctuation. The total of incurred losses is not a convenient base be-

TABLE 13

EXAMPLE OF GROUP HEALTH INCURRED AND
UNREPORTED LOSS RESERVE CALCULATION

Date (1)	Cash Claims Paid in Three Months Ending on Given Date (2)	Incurred and Unreported Claims on Given Date (3)	Ratio of Incurred and Unreported to Cash Claims Paid (3) ÷ (2)
12–31–1957	$2,040,100.50	$ 778,298.35	0.3815
12–31–1958	2,150,385.00	862,304.38	0.4010
12–31–1959	2,240,860.80	921,441.95	0.4112
12–31–1960	2,400,500.00	(1,008,210.00)	(0.4200)

cause losses incurred in the current year will not be known. The known-loss reserve could be used as a base, but any error it might contain would also produce an error in the reserve for incurred and unreported losses. For these reasons, losses paid during a three-month period are generally used in reserve calculation. Whatever the base, adjustments in the ratios may have to be made because of epidemics, changes in accounting time lags, and changes in proportions of business involving extended liability under state disability plans.[8]

Some companies employ a more detailed method to determine the reserve for incurred and unreported claims. This method is based upon a detailed analysis of reported claims in relation to the incurred dates of the claims.

Detailed statistics must be gathered over a period of time sufficient to allow claim reports to mature, and continuous rec-

---

[8] See Neumann, *op. cit.*, p. 204.

ords are kept showing reported dates for losses incurred each month. It may be found, for example, that 60 per cent of all claims incurred in December have been reported by December 31, that 80 per cent of all claims incurred in November have been reported by December 31, and so on.[9] An "unreported factor" for each month is then multiplied by the amount of reported claims for each incurred month to determine the amount of unreported claims.[10]

Loss Expense Reserve. Loss reserves provide only for future payment of incurred losses and allocated claim expense, but just as much a liability are the general claim settlement expenses that will accompany these future loss payments. The basis of determining the expense reserves is not designated by law, but the usual method of computing these reserves is to multiply loss reserves by a predetermined percentage. The size of the claim expense reserve in relation to the loss reserve is determined by past experience, with adjustments for cost trends and any changes in claims procedures.

Reserves for Extended Insurance Benefits

Special reserves are calculated to provide for the payment of claims arising under both the maternity and the nonmaternity "extended insurance benefits" provisions of group health insurance. Calculations are made separately for employees and dependents for each of the different extended benefits provided: three months nonmaternity extended hospital and surgical insurance, one or two years nonmaternity extended major medical insurance for disabled employees and dependents, and nine months extended hospital and surgical maternity benefits.

The reserves for nonmaternity extended insurance benefits

---

[9] For an excellent discussion of reserve calculation, see John Rowell, "Loss Reserve Calculation," *Proceedings of the Insurance Accounting and Statistical Association*, 1949. For a discussion of statistical methods of collecting data for reserve and premium calculation see Charles E. Probst, "Recent Developments in Group Accident and Health Statistical Procedure," *ibid.*, 1950.

[10] The "unreported factor" is determined by subtracting the figure 1 from the reciprocal of the decimal equivalent of the proportion of total claims reported.

are determined by relating claims of employees occurring during the extended insurance period from the beginning of a
given year, where the employee was first unable to work during
the previous year, to the total benefits in force at the end of
the previous year. Such ratios are usually calculated for three
years to minimize chance fluctuations, and the final ratio to be
used is multiplied by the total benefits in force at the end of
the current year. The reserve for dependent extended benefits
is determined by using the same ratio as that used for employees, since it is impossible to obtain the "first unable to
work" date for dependents. The ratio is applied to the total
dependent coverage in force but must be increased to allow
for an average number of dependents, since benefits in force
will reflect dependent units and not the actual number of dependents insured.[11]

By far the largest reserve required for extended benefits is
that for the nine-month extension of maternity and obstetrical
benefits. The reserves for maternity and obstetrical claims are
determined the same as the regular extension reserves by relating the claims for the first nine months of the current year
to an average of the total benefits in force during the last nine
months of the previous year, during which time conception
presumably occurred. The ratio thus obtained (usually from
three years of study) is then multiplied by the average benefits
in force during the last nine months of the current year.

All these extension reserves are set up on the assumption
that all insurance under policies containing such benefits is terminating on the annual statement date; therefore, the reserves
are not limited to the expected payments to be made in the
following year on actual terminations of insurance.[12] This is
done because these reserves are not loss reserves. They are actually unearned premium reserves, since the extended insurance benefits represent unexpired periods of protection for
certain claims.

---

[11] Neumann, *op. cit.*, p. 205.
[12] *Ibid.*

Contingency Reserves

Contingency reserves are established to allow for unusual occurrences, the possibility of upward trends in claim costs, and the possibility of a decline in premiums without a proportionate decline in potential liabilities.[13] Contingency reserves are generally considered purely voluntary allocation of unassigned surplus to represent a safety factor to meet any unfavorable circumstances that might arise.

However, the State of Missouri requires the accumulation of a contingency reserve for all group health business by companies doing business in that state. The ultimate amount of contingency reserve required is 50 per cent of a year's net premiums with the annual minimum contribution rate set at 2 per cent.[14] However, the annual contribution need not be more than 10 per cent of the amount necessary to reach the ultimate goal. In other words, after the reserve reaches 30 per cent of a year's net premiums, the rate can be less than 2 per cent annually.

Special Reserves

In addition to the reserves discussed above, two others may be established by group companies when applicable. One of these is for reinsurance, and the other is for assessments under state disability plans.

Reinsurance Reserve. There is very little reinsurance in the usual sense in group health, because there is very little catastrophe hazard. Most reinsurance arises from the sharing of a large group by two or more companies, with one company acting as the insurer, providing the policy and all service, and the others acting as reinsurers. Where such reinsurance exists, each company involved must add to or subtract from its total reserve liability (calculated on the usual basis of direct insur-

---

[13] The last refers to state disability plans, where premiums are based on current wages while benefits are related to wages during a base period. If wages decline, the premium base declines before the decline occurs in the benefit base.

[14] *Missouri Departmental Order #38,* December 15, 1951.

ance in force) the amount necessary to reflect the additional or reduced liability. The individual reserve items for reinsurance are calculated in the same manner as the reserves discussed throughout this chapter. For reinsurance ceded, the reserve items are subtracted from the total reserve liability to obtain the aggregate net liability. For reinsurance accepted, the reinsurance reserves are added to obtain aggregate reserve liability.

Reserves for Assessments. Reserves for assessments are required for companies writing the statutory benefits under state disability plans. One such reserve covers the insurer's contribution to administrative expense of state funds and supervision of private plans; the other reserve covers the insurer's liability to the state fund for disability benefits to the unemployed. Both are prescribed annually by the states on the basis of total taxable payrolls of the groups insured by each insurer.

CONTRACT-YEAR RESERVES

Not only must an insurer calculate its reserve liabilities for annual statement purposes, but it must also charge each policyholder with a share of these liabilities at the end of each contract year before retroactive rate reductions can be made. The objective of this procedure is, of course, to retain funds from policyholders to correspond to aggregate liabilities of the insurer under group health policies.

No unearned premium reserve is necessary unless premiums have been paid in advance; but in the rate adjustment formula, each group must be charged with reserves for losses, loss expenses, extended insurance benefits, contingencies, and perhaps reinsurance and assessments. The general principles, general studies, ratios, or factors used for calculating statement reserves may also be used for contract-year reserves, but some modifications are necessary. The following discussion deals with the differences between calculating statement reserves and contract-year reserves.

Loss Reserves

The general type of study used for statement reserves is also used for contract-year reserves, with the studies made on a year-round basis to allow for seasonal variation in claims and reporting lags. If an average value is used for known losses, allowance must be made for variations in types of coverage for specific groups from the types of coverage comprising total insurance in force. For unknown losses or a combined calculation of known and unknown, reserve calculation must allow for lags and claim reporting patterns of each specific group.

In event of policy cancellation there are two methods of treating loss reserves. Under the first the company establishes the reserve for the sole purpose of paying claims. If claims prove less than the reserve, there is no refund to the policyholder. Under the second the reserve is returned entirely to the policyholder through claims and a dividend of any unpaid balance. A company using the second method must increase all loss reserves considerably, because the averaging technique between different groups is lost. For example, assume two terminating groups, each with a loss reserve of $100,000. If one group has losses of $95,000, and the other develops losses of $105,000, the insurer has exactly broken even if there is no refund of reserve balances. Under the second method the insurer would have lost $5,000 unless all reserves had been increased to compensate for the loss of salvage from overestimates of reserve liabilities under terminated contracts.

Reserves for Extended Insurance Benefits

The regular extension liabilities for a specific group may be calculated by using the same ratios used in calculating statement liabilities, since premiums for specific groups will reflect variation from the average benefit level. However, liability under extended maternity benefits is usually calculated by a more direct method. It is relatively simple to ascertain the total annual premium paid for maternity benefits for an individual group. The usual practice is to reserve 75 per cent of total annual premiums for maternity coverage. This accurately reflects potential liabilities extending nine months beyond the end of the contract year—assuming, of course, that premium rates are accurate. Actually, the reserve can be less than 75 per cent of annual gross premium, since commissions, taxes, and other expenses have already been incurred.

Contingency Reserve

Each policyholder is charged with a share of the statutory or voluntary contingency reserve. The statutory percentage is modified to allow for dividends, since the requirement is based on net premiums and not gross. The contingency reserve for a given group may be increased to allow a reserve item for chance fluctuation of morbidity for the group, or this reserve item may be treated separately in the retroactive adjustment formula.

CRITIQUE

The broad objectives of reserves are clear enough: sufficient funds on hand to discharge all obligations. Unfortunately from the standpoint of administration, there is no simple or convenient basis upon which to establish these reserves, except for the unearned premium reserve. Other reserves are determined by the companies themselves and by their own judgment. The state insurance departments can do little more than make periodic evaluations of the reserve estimates made by the companies themselves.

The problem of reserve adequacy cannot be divorced from the question of premium adequacy. The need for conservatism in reserves is recognized by responsible industry men, but rate levels for the past several years have contained no margin for adequate contingency reserves.[15] The fact that there seems to be no effective method of direct rate regulation is a strong

---

[15] See Chapter XII.

argument in favor of indirect rate regulation through the requirement of conservative contingency reserves.

The Missouri requirement of contingency reserves represents recognition by one regulatory authority of a need for conservatism. The Missouri method, in effect, establishes minimum rates that vary by insurer, since each insurer over a period must discharge its current obligations from premium income and retain sufficient funds to match its statutory contingent liability.

Since the Missouri reserve requirement is based on net rather than gross or manual premiums, the statutory reserve requirement for a given amount of exposure is generally larger if the exposure is in a small rather than a large group. That is, requiring a reserve that is a given percentage of net premiums has a greater relative effect on small groups than on large groups because each group is charged with its contribution to contingency reserves in retroactive rate adjustment formulas, and rates per unit of exposure are reduced for the larger groups through the volume discount factor.

It would seem logical to establish the same contingency reserve for exposure of 1,000 lives under a given benefit plan, regardless of whether these lives are insured under a single group contract or several. If this is true, reserve requirements should then be based on exposure and not on net premiums. An equitable and relatively convenient base for measuring this exposure would be manual premiums. Gross premiums should not be used as the base, because prospective rate adjustments and the volume discount would make the base vary by size of group and not directly by units of exposure.

CHAPTER X

SELF-REGULATION

MANY aspects of group health insurance have become standardized or made relatively uniform by co-operative effort of insurers writing such coverage. Much standardization would have come sooner or later without any outside motivating factors, but at least part of the recent co-operative effort is a result of some serious problems facing health insurance. Among these problems facing insurers are poor underwriting results, the threat of federal entry into the health insurance field, and state legislative activity, especially in the field of requiring convertibility of group health insurance coverage.

The most important organizations for self-regulation of health insurance are discussed below, and each of these is involved in group health insurance although their activities are not limited to group insurance alone. Specific areas of self-regulation will be discussed under the headings of the organizations that make the self-regulation possible.

HEALTH INSURANCE COUNCIL

The Health Insurance Council was organized in 1946 at the suggestion of the president of the American Medical Association, and it was chartered for the specific purpose of bringing about closer relations between insurers, hospitals, and doctors.[1] Today the Council is composed of the member companies of the following eight trade associations: (1) American Life Convention, (2) American Mutual Insurance Alliance,

---

[1] See E. J. Faulkner, address at Group Insurance Forum, Health Insurance Association of America, February 10, 1960.

(3) Association of Casualty and Surety Companies, (4) Association of Life Insurance Medical Directors, (5) Health Insurance Association of America, (6) International Claim Association, (7) Life Insurance Association of America, and (8) Life Insurers Conference.

To carry out its original purpose, the Council now operates through a system of committees under the general direction of a central committee composed of the board of directors of the Council. The areas of primary interest of the Council are discussed below under the headings of the principal standing committees.

Medical Relations Committee

This committee works with physicians and the various medical organizations in an attempt to discuss and resolve the problems arising out of the relationship of insurance to medicine. This Committee, working with the Uniform Forms Committee, has made excellent progress in securing the support of doctors and medical societies for standardized claim forms and prompt claim reporting. Much has been done also to promote awareness among physicians of the problems of consistently rising medical costs. Many county medical societies have established review committees to co-operate with insurers in arbitrating charges considered excessive by the insurer. In turn, insurers have made their own claims experience available to local medical societies to assist them in their attempts to develop relative value schedules.

Hospital Relations Committee

This committee works with hospitals in much the same way the Medical Relations Committee works with physicians, to resolve the important problems involved in the relationship of private carrier insurance and the provision of hospital care. Activities of this Committee are many and varied, but probably the most important development has been the Hospital Admission Plans (discussed in Chapter VI) which make it possible for the hospital to grant the insured patient immediate admission and discharge credit for hospitalization insurance.

Uniform Forms Committee

This Committee has been successful in securing the support of both the American Medical Association and the American Hospital Association of uniform claim and underwriting forms developed by the Committee. This development has special significance in placing private carriers, who previously had a multiplicity of claim forms, at a more equal competitive position with Blue Cross and Blue Shield with respect to ease of claims processing by both hospitals and physicians.

Technical Advisory Committee

The Technical Advisory Committee works with other standing committees of the Council and with the various state subcommittees in a number of areas. These areas include studies of overinsurance, duplications of coverage, claims cost control, and the annual survey of voluntary health insurance coverage.

Allied Health Services

This committee works with a number of groups whose specialties give them an important and direct interest in the private provision and financing of health care. These groups include public health administrators, blood banks, chiropractors, Christian Science practitioners, dentists, homemakers, naturopaths, nurses, nursing home operators, optometrists, pharmacists, podiatrists, and psychologists.

HEALTH INSURANCE ASSOCIATION OF AMERICA

For more than half a century, different segments of the health insurance business were represented by two different trade associations: the Bureau of Accident and Health Underwriters, and the Health and Accident Underwriters Conference. In 1956 these two organizations were succeeded by the Health Insurance Association of America. Membership in the Association in 1961 numbered about three hundred health insurance companies of all types. The work of the Association is carried on by its board of directors, a full-time staff, and a large number of committees.

The services of the Association will be discussed below under five main headings: (1) legislative activities, (2) standards of conduct, (3) information and research, (4) company relations, and (5) public relations.[2]

Legislative Activities

The Association conducts a continuing study of both state and federal legislation affecting health insurance, and member companies are informed of legislative activities through periodic bulletins and reports. Officers of member companies work closely with legislators and government administrative officials in connection with all legislation and insurance department rulings affecting the health insurance business.

The Association works closely with the National Association of Insurance Commissioners for the purpose of developing and promoting the adoption of model legislation, such as the Model Group Accident and Sickness Insurance Bill reproduced in Appendix A.

Standards of Conduct

The members of the HIAA adopted unanimously in 1957 a code of ethical standards for the guidance of members, and continued membership in the Association is conditioned upon adherence to the code. Under this code, each member company pledges itself:

1. To offer only insurance providing effective and real protection against such loss as the policy is designed to cover.
2. To write its policies in clear and direct language without unreasonable restrictions and limitations.
3. To advertise its policies in such manner that the public can readily understand the protection offered, and not use advertising which has the tendency or capacity to mislead or deceive.

---

[2] See Health Insurance Association of America, *Annual Report*, 1959.

4. To select, train, and supervise personnel of integrity in a manner which will assure intelligent, honest, and courteous sales and service.
5. To engage only in sales methods, promotional practices and other transactions which give primary consideration to the needs, interest, and continued satisfaction of the persons insured.
6. To endeavor to establish the insurability of persons at the time of application in every instance where such insurability is a factor in the issuance or continuance of the insurance or in the liability of the insurer.
7. To pay all just claims fairly, courteously, and promptly, with a minimum of requirements.
8. To continue research and experimentation in order to meet the changing needs of the public.
9. To engage in keen, fair competition, so the public may obtain the protection it needs at a reasonable price.

The significance of the code is best appreciated when it is understood that members of the HIAA write over 85 per cent of the health insurance in the United States.

In the 1950's there was an increasing interest in all quarters in the problem of providing and continuing coverage for older citizens, especially those retired. State legislative activities centered mainly on conversion privileges of group insurance and guaranteed renewability of coverage, while federal activities centered on providing a government system of health care protection for the aged. This legislative pressure and awareness by responsible health insurance officials that private insurance has not yet reached its full potential, have produced concerted efforts in the direction of providing medical care coverage for the older citizen. It has been stated more than once that the individual company may have a choice on providing and continuing coverage for the elderly but that the entire private health insurance industry has no such choice.[3]

At a special meeting December 8, 1958, the HIAA adopted a resolution on health insurance for the elderly and otherwise poorer risks. In this resolution each member company is asked

---

[3] Travis T. Wallace, presidential address at annual meeting of the Health Insurance Association of America, May 4, 1959.

to consider carefully and independently the implementation of the following recommendations:

1. Insurers offering individual and family coverage of the cost of health care under contracts which are renewable at the option of the insurer should continue and accelerate their progress in minimizing the refusal of renewal solely because of deterioration of health after issuance.

2. Every insurer offering health care coverages should, among the types of insurance contracts it offers, promptly make available to insurable adults policies which are guaranteed renewable for life.

3. Every insurer should develop sales programs designed to encourage the sale of permanent health care insurance where the need for this type of coverage exists.

4. Every insurer offering individual and family hospital, surgical, and medical care coverages should promptly take steps if it is not presently doing so to offer insurance coverage to persons now over age 65.

5. It is essential that adequate voluntary health insurance be available to broad classes of physically impaired people. Initial insurance underwriting standards essential to fulfilling the first two of these recommendations increase the need for insurance for the physically impaired. Otherwise, in the future these people may be deprived of insurance coverage. It is recommended that each company carefully consider how it can contribute to the achievement of this objective.

6. Every insurer writing coverage on a group basis should develop and aggressively promote soundly financed coverages that will continue after retirement.

7. Every insurer offering coverage on a group basis should encourage the inclusion in the group contract of the right to convert to an individual contract on termination of employment.

Many private and association carriers in recent years have aggressively offered individual health coverage to persons over age 65, and many have permitted retired employees to continue group coverage after retirement. A growing number of private and association carriers permit conversion of group coverage to individuals regardless of the reason for terminating group insurance. Many companies make no charge against the group plan for conversions of medical expense reimbursement coverage, but most of these reserve the right to do so in the future if necessary.[4]

---

[4] See discussion by E. Earl Ward, *Transactions of the Society of Actuaries,* Vol. 11 (1959), p. 478.

Because costs under major and comprehensive medical plans rise sharply with age, some group men have felt that an average term insurance premium for such plans is not feasible if coverage is to be continued for retired employees without drastic reduction in benefits.[5] However, some companies are experimenting with the pre-funding of health insurance costs for those retired through a system similar to a deposit administration pension plan. One group authority suggests that the costs of pre-funding health care is relatively small compared to the cost of funding a reasonable pension.[6]

Information and Research

The HIAA carries on an extensive program of research through the division of Information and Research. This division compiles and evaluates insurer experience with various kinds of risks, experiments with new types of benefits, and methods of doing business. The subjects of such research also include claims cost control, overinsurance, duplications of insurance, insurance of older citizens, statistical programs, reserve valuation, and foreign and domestic government-sponsored insurance plans.

The division distributes information gathered to member companies through periodic bulletins and special reports.

Company Relations

The principal purpose of the Company Relations Division of the HIAA is to serve as a central channel of communication by which member companies may keep abreast of changing underwriting and marketing practices. This purpose is accomplished through special health insurance forums, a weekly newsletter, periodic bulletins, and the sponsorship of an educational course for home office employees.

Public Relations

Public relations activities of the HIAA are carried on through the Health Insurance Institute, which is under the di-

[5] Arthur G. Weaver, "Group Insurance For Retired Lives," *Proceedings, Bureau-Conference Group A & H Meeting,* February 7–9, 1955, p. 49.

[6] See discussion by Morton D. Miller, *Transactions of the Society of Actuaries,* Vol. 11 (1959), p. 525.

rection of a committee elected by the membership of the HIAA. Although the HIAA provides the total financing for the Institute, the Institute operates and is identified separately from the Association. The Institute works closely with the Institute of Life Insurance and the Health Insurance Council, and its principal activity has been directed toward developing better public understanding and strengthening public confidence in health insurance.[7]

In carrying out its principal objective, the Institute provides three general types of service. The first of these involves periodic reports to insurers of trends in public thinking, as reflected in the press, organized surveys, and special reports from such groups as organized labor, doctors, hospital administrators, and social welfare experts. The second general type of service involves releasing health information to the general public, including the annual publication of a health insurance fact book similar to the well-known *Life Insurance Fact Book* published by the Institute of Life Insurance. In addition, the Institute publishes a bimonthly "Health Insurance News" release sent to the daily and weekly press, magazines, feature and science editors, hospital and medical publications, insurance and employer magazines, the labor press, and columnists.

The third service of the Institute concerns more direct dealings with specific segments of the population. Special booklets, filmstrips, and policy kits are furnished to educators for use in classes in both colleges and secondary schools. Many other special services are provided in connection with the national work of the Health Insurance Council.

CANADIAN ASSOCIATIONS

Organization of insurance companies in Canada for the purpose of co-operative effort has been much behind that in the United States. This is no doubt partly because, in the health insurance field, premium volume is relatively small compared

---

[7] See Health Insurance Association of America, *Annual Report,* 1959, pp. 32–41.

to the volume in the United States. It may also be partly because health insurance in Canada is divided among Canadian, British, and United States companies, so organization many years ago did not seem feasible.

Life insurance companies in Canada are represented by the Canadian Life Insurance Officers Association, while casualty companies are represented by the All Canada Insurance Federation. However, some major companies in the health insurance field have not been members of either association.[8] Lack of unified action made it impossible for health insurance companies in Canada to wage an effective campaign against the adoption of the provincial health plans.

To achieve some unity of action, the two associations discussed above formed a Joint Committee on Health Insurance in 1953. This Committee recommended early in 1959 that a single organization be formed to represent the entire health insurance industry in Canada. A meeting was held in June, 1959, to form the Canadian Health Insurance Association, to serve the industry in Canada much the same as the HIAA serves in the United States.

---

[8] See W. Douglas Bell, "New Developments in Canadian Health Insurance," address at annual meeting of the Health Insurance Association of America, May 6, 1959.

CHAPTER XI

GOVERNMENTAL REGULATION

THE objectives of insurance regulation may be said to include protection of policyholders, production of revenue, and retaliation against discrimination by one state against companies domiciled in another. Revenue and retaliation are of course of general interest, but the discussion in this chapter will deal only with the regulation of the health insurance business as it affects those insured. Some regulation, including that of reserves and legal definitions of group health insurance, was discussed in earlier chapters.

RATE REGULATION

The primary purpose of rate regulation is to provide rates that are adequate, reasonable, and nondiscriminatory. Group health rates are excluded from regulation under the all-industry casualty and surety rate laws and from the provisions of the early All-Industry Accident and Health Bill. However, group health rates are not entirely free from regulation.

The New York insurance law requires that no group health policy may be issued within or outside the state by a company doing business in New York unless it appears to be "self-supporting on reasonable assumptions as to morbidity or other appropriate claim rate, interest, and expense." The superintendent of insurance is empowered to require the companies to submit directly or through an approved organization their experience and other information necessary to evaluate the premium rates. A schedule of initial premium rates, classification of risks, and maximum commissions payable for acquisition are required to be filed with the New York superintendent of insurance. Companies are prohibited from issuing policies for which the first year's premium is below that indicated by the schedules on file, or to pay higher commissions (or any other fees) than those filed. The superintendent is empowered to set minimum rates, after a hearing, where initial rates for any cover appear to be too low.

While New York regulation is aimed primarily at minimum rates, California aims the regulation at maximum rates by requiring that "rates must be reasonable in relation to benefits." However, all attempts at regulating group health rates have been limited to regulating initial rates only. The effect of New York regulation of initial rates is of course felt nation-wide, since the regulation applies to all business written anywhere by companies doing business in New York. Companies operating in New York write a large part of total group volume, and the desire to avoid a minimum rate has led companies to attempt to keep initial rates reasonably adequate. Companies not operating in New York are not affected by the New York regulation, and they continue to set initial rates at whatever level is required to compete for business.

No minimum initial rate has been established for covers in New York for two main reasons. First, the Insurance Department has no more knowledge than have the companies as to just where minimum rates should be set. Second, a minimum initial rate applied to New York companies would place them in a poor competitive position in other states where they could be underbid by companies not affected by minimum rate requirements.

There has been no general requirement that companies submit their experience in order that initial rates might be evaluated by the Insurance Department of New York, but in a few instances companies have been asked to justify initial rates that appeared to be out of line. The result has been a greater uniformity of initial rates in New York than in other states.

The power to set minimum initial rates has definitely been important in preventing serious initial rate wars, particularly for the larger groups. Rate competition for these groups has been fierce, but minimum initial rate regulatory authority has no doubt kept it from becoming more serious.

Rates for group health insurance are required to be filed in less than half the states; but even where filing is required, filing means little since the commissioners have little or no basis for criticizing or refusing to approve the rates. Limited regulation of initial rates and the absence of regulation of renewal rates add to a very primitive form of rate regulation in group health insurance. Even in jurisdictions where Blue Cross–Blue Shield associations must secure permission for rate increases, regulatory authorities have no better information than the associations as to what rate levels should be.

None of the foregoing is meant to imply that better methods of rate regulation are necessarily available, and reasons have already been discussed for the absence of strong initial rate regulation. There are additional reasons why renewal rates cannot be effectively regulated.

No system of group health rate calculation (and thus regulation) can make allowance for all the factors which will affect claim costs. Attempts have been made to determine the effect of industry, age, sex, income, and geographical location on claim costs. To the extent that the effect of these factors is predictable, renewal rates are approximately the same as initial rates. However, the effects of many factors can only be measured in retrospect. No system of rate calculation or regulation can make accurate allowance for the following factors known to affect claim costs:

1. The underwriting practices of the particular group company.
2. The effects of policyholder personnel practices on the quality of the labor force.
3. The policyholder's contribution to premiums and the attendant interest in claims control.
4. The general attitude of the employees of a particular policyholder toward health insurance.

If no workable system of direct rate regulation can be devised, it seems logical that some other approach could be used. Requirement of adequate reserves could solve the problem of rate adequacy for both initial and renewal rates, since a deficit would appear earlier under a given rate level. Reserve requirements based on exposure, not premiums, and a modification of retroactive rate adjustments could solve the problem of equity.

The problem in recent years for insurers has been that rates in general have not been adequate to meet losses and expenses after retroactive rate adjustments to the better groups. The ordinary legal requirement of adequacy of premiums is for the protection of the general public against insurer insolvency, so it is most fortunate for the general public that the majority of group health insurance is written by companies in no danger of becoming insolvent.

FAIR TRADE PRACTICES

In 1944 the United States Supreme Court held insurance to be commerce in the South-Eastern Underwriters Association case, and therefore subject to all the Federal antitrust laws when transacted interstate. Following the enactment of the McCarran-Ferguson Act [1] a year later, Congress declared insurance to be free from federal regulation, "except to the extent that insurance is not regulated by state law." The McCarran-Ferguson Act led to the formation of all-industry committees in the insurance industry to work with the National Association of Insurance Commissioners in securing national and reasonably uniform state insurance regulation.

Among the results of the co-operation of the committees and the NAIC, is found the All-Industry Fair Trade Practices Act. This act has now been adopted in all states and the commonwealth of Puerto Rico. This law specifically defines certain acts and practices as either unfair methods of competition or as deceptive and unfair acts. Insurance commissioners were empowered to issue cease-and-desist orders to insurers guilty of

---

[1] Public Law 15, 79th Cong., 1st sess.

such acts as: (1) misrepresentations and false advertising of policy contracts, (2) defamation, (3) boycott, (4) coercion, (5) intimidation, (6) false financial statements, (7) offerings of stock or contracts promising profits as inducements to insure, (8) unfair discrimination, and (9) rebating.

A second section of the Act recognizes that it is impossible to define all unfair methods of competition and all unfair and deceptive acts, and therefore gives the commissioner authority to bring action when it appears that an insurer is guilty of unfair competition or any unfair or deceptive practices.

As a guide to what constitutes an unfair trade practice, the National Association of Insurance Commissioners adopted a code of health insurance advertising rules in 1955, and about two thirds of the states have adopted this code.

The Federal Trade Commission code dealing with advertising by mail-order insurers was the first attempt of the Commission to regulate specific insurer conduct, other than actions regarding coercion and boycott which had not been removed from federal jurisdiction by the McCarran-Ferguson Act. In 1954 and 1955 the FTC issued formal complaints against forty-one insurance companies allegedly using false or deceptive advertising. The companies, with the support of the trade associations and the National Association of Insurance Commissioners, presented the following defenses: (1) the complaints were based on advertising two years old which had since been abandoned; (2) there was no evidence that applicants had been misled; (3) the advertising was regulated by state law, and the FTC therefore had no jurisdiction; (4) the statements were misleading only when quoted out of context; and (5) there had been no intention to mislead the insuring public.

In the two leading cases (National Casualty Company, and American Hospital and Life Insurance Company) the charges were dismissed by the United States Supreme Court on June 30, 1958.[2] In several other cases the Supreme Court refused to

---

[2] Health Insurance Association of America, *Annual Report, 1959*, Appendix A.

review (*certiorari* denied) the decisions of the Circuit Courts. In the others the FTC dismissed the cases or dropped them with a consent order. Regulation of advertising and unfair trade practices in general thus appears to rest in the hands of the states for the time being.

CONTINUANCE OF COVERAGE

Several states, including New York, have enacted legislation concerning the renewability (or noncancellability) of individual policies and the conversion of group health insurance policies. Regulations concerning individual policies (which would include converted group coverage) sharply restrict the insurer's right to refuse contract renewal.

With the adoption of the so-called "Metcalf Bill" in 1958, New York required group insurance companies, at the option of the group policyholder, to include a conversion privilege in all group medical expense reimbursement policies. This law was modified in 1960 and made mandatory for all such policies issued or changed after January 1, 1961.[3]

As modified, the law requires a guarantee to the employee that he can convert to individual coverage regardless of the reason for terminating employment or union membership, provided the employee had been insured under the group plan for at least three months. At the election of the employee, eligible dependents insured under the group plan must be included in the converted policy, but maternity benefits are not required to be included. The conversion privilege is also available to the surviving spouse and insured dependent children of an employee who dies while covered by the group plan.

Under the 1958 law a minimum level of benefits was prescribed for the converted policy, but under the 1960 revision the person eligible can select from three levels of benefit as long as benefits selected do not exceed those of the group plan. The superintendent of insurance is given power under the

---

[3] Chapter 820, New York Laws of 1960, generally called the Russo Bill.

1960 law to set maximum rates for policy conversion by persons age 60 or over, provided they have been insured by the group plan for at least two years. The 1960 law provides that no age limitation may be placed on the exercise of the conversion privilege.

FEDERAL TAXATION OF PREMIUMS AND BENEFITS

Both premiums and benefits under group health insurance enjoy special federal tax treatment making valuable fringe benefits from the standpoint of both the employer and employee.[4]

Premiums

Premium contributions paid by an employer for employees' group health insurance are deductible from gross income, provided they are reasonable in amount and represent an "ordinary and necessary" business expense. Such premiums paid by the employer for any form of group health insurance do not represent taxable income to the employees.

Premium contributions made by the employee for income reimbursement coverage, including the accidental death and dismemberment cover, are not deductible on the employee's individual income tax return. However, employee contributions for all forms of group medical reimbursement coverage are deductible from adjusted gross income as medical expense, if the employee itemizes his deductions. This deduction is of course subject to the general rule that medical expenses are deductible only to the extent to which they exceed 3 per cent of adjusted gross income of the taxpayer.

Benefits

Amounts paid to an employee for dismemberment under the accidental death and dismemberment cover do not represent taxable income to the employee, regardless of who pays the

---

[4] I.R.C. of 1954, Secs. 104, 105, 106, 162, and 213, and applicable regulations.

premiums for the coverage. Death benefits under this cover are subject to the same rules as those applying to group term life insurance and do not represent taxable income to the beneficiary, although they are subject to the federal estate tax.

Benefits received by an employee under income reimbursement coverage may be at least in part subject to federal income tax. The portion of such benefits attributable to the employee's own contributions do not represent taxable income to the employee, but benefits attributable to employer contributions are subject to special rules. All amounts in excess of $100 per week due to employer contributions represent fully taxable income to the employee. The first $100 per week of benefit due to employer contributions is excludable from gross income by the employee, but only up to retirement age. However, during the first week of disability the first $100 from employer contributions is excludable only if the disability is due to bodily injury or if the taxpayer is hospitalized for one full day during his period of sickness.

Medical expense reimbursement benefits do not represent taxable income to the employee regardless of who pays the premiums, except to the extent that these benefits represent reimbursement for medical expenses deducted for income tax purposes in a prior year. However, amounts received as reimbursement for expenses incurred in the current year must be offset against otherwise deductible medical expenses, if the employee itemizes his deductions from adjusted gross income.

The rules discussed above for both premiums and benefits apply to sole proprietorships and partnerships as well as corporations. However, there is no employer-employee relationship in sole proprietorships or partnerships as between the firm itself and the sole proprietor or partners.

Sole proprietors must file the usual individual return, and they are permitted to deduct from gross income the premiums paid for employees' group health insurance. With respect to premiums and benefits of the sole proprietor's own insurance, the rules discussed above concerning the employee's own contributions apply.

Partners in a partnership also must file separate individual returns, because the firm files only an "information" return. On their individual returns, partners treat their own insurance and benefits the same as does the sole proprietor.

IMPACT OF GOVERNMENTAL REGULATION

Group health insurers are subject to regulation in some areas other than those discussed above. Most states have adopted the Unauthorized Insurers Service of Process Act recommended by an all-industry committee and the National Association of Insurance Commissioners. Many states require filing of group health policies and prescribe some standard policy provisions. The latter usually include such subjects as: (1) provision for issuing certificates to employees, (2) provision that statements are representations and not warranties, (3) rules concerning remittance of premiums, (4) provision for adding new employees, and (5) provisions for dealing with proofs of loss and payment of claims.

Regulations such as these cause no injury to group insurers, except in administrative expense and confusion. To the extent that state laws are not uniform on policy provisions, the insurer must maintain a multiplicity of forms or endorsements to be able to comply with regulations in all states where they operate. There have been instances of delays in accepting policy filings which caused real inconvenience to the insurer.

The purpose of regulation requiring a conversion privilege in group contracts and the restriction of the cancellation privilege in individual policies is certainly easy to identify. Legislators are attempting to secure for citizens of their own states more security on continuance of coverage at older ages or after deterioration of health. The motive is certainly commendable, but such a move may severely hamper private insurers in their attempts to solve the problem on a soundly financed basis.

Proposals of various kinds at each session of the state legislatures present group health insurers with what amounts almost to a "brush fire" type of threat to their own efficient national operation. Continued scattered and varied regulations would seem to be so harmful to legitimate experimentation with solutions to national health insurance problems that legislators should be content to give more attention to joint recommendations of the industry and the National Association of Insurance Commissioners. Failure to secure more uniformity may eventually pave the way for a system of broad federal regulation superimposed on that of the states.

CHAPTER XII

PROBLEMS AND ISSUES

SOME of the rating, reserve, regulation, and competition problems of the group health insurance business have been discussed in earlier chapters. A number of significant problems and issues seemed important enough to warrant separate discussion, and the purpose of this chapter is to examine in detail those problems and issues common to all types of group health insurers.

UNDERWRITING RESULTS

Probably the most serious problem to face group insurers in recent years has been the upward trend of both loss ratios (the ratio of losses to premiums earned) and combined loss and expense ratios (the ratio of combined losses and expenses to premiums earned). Table 14 shows these ratios for all private stock and mutual companies combined and the same ratios for the eight largest private group health companies for 1947 through 1959. The ratios are for all group health lines combined, because during World War II the major group companies discontinued calculating these ratios for individual lines due to the expense involved.

The loss and combined ratios for all reporting companies for 1947 through 1950 are based on earned premiums before mutual company dividends, while both ratios for 1951 through 1959 are based on earned premiums after mutual company dividends. The ratios for the two periods therefore are not strictly comparable, and this accounts for a large part of the increase in both ratios from 1950 to 1951. The ratios for the eight largest companies, which write over 60 per cent of all private carrier group health premiums, are comparable throughout the period, because all are based on premiums after mutual company dividends.

For all reporting companies, both the loss and combined ratios increased consistently from 1948 to a peak in 1951, while both ratios declined temporarily from 1952 to 1954. Higher

TABLE 14

<small>GROUP HEALTH RATIOS OF LOSSES INCURRED TO PREMIUMS EARNED AND COMBINED LOSSES AND EXPENSES INCURRED TO PREMIUMS EARNED FOR ALL REPORTING COMPANIES AND EIGHT LARGEST GROUP HEALTH COMPANIES, 1947–59</small>

	Combined Loss and Expense Ratios*		Loss Ratios*	
Years	All Reporting Companies	Eight Largest Companies	All Reporting Companies	Eight Largest Companies
1959	101.2	101.1	87.8	90.4
1958	101.1	100.4	87.6	89.5
1957	101.5	100.9	88.3	90.5
1956	99.5	100.1	86.5	89.6
1955	98.4	98.9	86.2	87.5
1954	96.9	97.1	84.1	86.7
1953	98.7	99.1	85.6	88.3
1952	100.0	99.7	86.4	88.7
1951	101.1	101.7	86.6	89.5
1950	92.5	97.7	75.3	83.1
1949	88.8	97.1	71.6	81.7
1948	85.8	93.9	68.4	78.0
1947	86.1	93.9	68.4	76.2

* Ratios of incurred losses and expenses to premiums earned.
Source: The figures were derived from Alfred M. Best Company, *Fire and Casualty Aggregates and Averages*, 1954; The Spectator Company, *Accident Insurance Register*, 1951–60; and the National Underwriter Company, *Argus Charts*, 1948–55.

loss ratios during the early part of the period shown in Table 14 were offset partially in final underwriting results by reductions in expense rates. The reduction in expense ratios (not shown separately) during the period was from 17.7 per cent in 1947 to 12.8 per cent in 1954. However, the expense ratio was reduced only slightly from 1954 to 1959, indicating some practical minimum to expense ratios if insurers are to provide the necessary service to policyholders.

In spite of consistently declining expense ratios after 1947, final underwriting results grew progressively worse until underwriting losses were suffered in 1951. The increasingly poor underwriting results during this period were due not only to rising claim costs but also to reduced premiums.[1]

There was a general upward revision of premium rates in the summer of 1952, and this upward revision was no doubt the principal reason for temporary improvement in underwriting results after the poor results in 1951. Practically all groups had completed at least one contract year under the higher rate level by the middle of 1954, so further improvement in 1955 could not be expected. The 1952 rates produced higher loss ratios in 1955 because of the continued upward trend in claim costs.[2]

The intercompany studies discussed in Chapter VII revealed clearly that claim costs were rising for medical care insurance, even though income reimbursement claim costs dropped consistently from 1947 to 1951. Full employment and high wages during this period were the principal reasons for the reduction in claim costs for income reimbursement insurance.[3] Four broad reasons have been given for the increase of medical care costs during this period.[4]

1. Higher claim frequencies probably account for a good part of the increased costs under medical care insurance. Higher claim frequencies for all basic medical care covers may be due in part to the many marginal workers employed after World War II. These marginal workers have included many married women and others not ordinarily in the labor market during less than full employment.

---

[1] Morton D. Miller, "Claim Trends in Group Accident and Health Insurance Indicates Operations Should Be Reviewed," address at Educational Seminar, Bureau of Accident and Health Underwriters reported in *Weekly Underwriter*, March 29, 1952.

[2] See Table 11, page 146.

[3] See discussion by J. H. Smith, A. G. Weaver, P. A. Rabenau, and G. S. Bere, *Transactions of the Society of Actuaries*, Vol. 4 (1952), p. 19 ff.

[4] Miller, *op. cit.*

2. A greater awareness of insurance benefits, coupled with the idea that insurance benefits are an integral part of wages, has no doubt been important in causing claim costs to increase. Duplication of insurance with Blue Cross and Blue Shield or individual commercial policies has made it attractive in many instances to "clean up" all physical infirmities regardless of nature or severity.

3. Inflation has had a serious impact on the costs under medical care insurance. The costs of medical care facilities have risen and there no longer remains any "salvage" on reimbursement type benefits. Rarely indeed will a daily room charge by a hospital be less than the maximum allowed under a hospitalization policy. Levels of room and board benefit that once provided for private or semiprivate care now provide for ward service only. Inflated costs of ancillary services mean that the blanket amounts allowed for such services are frequently entirely exhausted. Increased limits that companies allow for such services no doubt increase the tendency to "use" insurance benefits, since the very presence of insurance in substantial amounts tends to increase insurance use.

4. Both medical care policies and underwriting practices have been liberalized since World War II. Surgical schedules have been broadened to include "any cutting operation," and this has led inevitably to the payment of claims for procedures somewhere between medicine and dentistry. Age limits for dependent children have been broadened, the required minimum number of hours of hospital confinement has been reduced or removed, and benefits have been provided for anesthetics and out-patient services. All these result in higher claim costs, because they increase both the number and amount of claims.

The introduction of trustee, association, and union groups is an indication of the liberalization of underwriting practices. For groups of all types, there was a tendency for a period following World War II to look more at the size of the group and its potential premium than at the potential losses. The desire for volume was strong, and large transfer groups often were accepted with complete disregard for the experience of the previous carrier.

The reasons cited above for increased medical costs are still appropriate today, and an increase in the frequency of employee maternity claims reflects the greater proportion of working wives in the labor force.[5] The increase in major and comprehensive medical insurance has even made the tendency to "use" insurance benefits much worse, and this has been particularly true of plans providing a substantial "full-coverage" area without any use of coinsurance or deductible amount.[6]

Average hospital claim duration declined between 1950 and 1957, but this was due to new and improved medical techniques, the use of modern (and often expensive) drugs, and a substantial increase in confinement frequency for minor ailments and diagnosis.[7]

Claim costs are not a function of premium rate levels, but loss ratios are determined by both claim costs and premium levels. When claim costs rise, increased premium rates could keep loss and combined loss and expense ratios down, assuming of course that higher rate levels do not lead to lower quality business. It is evident from the figures in Table 12–1 that rate levels have not been adjusted rapidly enough to match higher claim costs. This lack of adjustment is due at least in part to many unsoundly designed comprehensive plans, too much optimism in the past on transfer business, and the continued practice of making refunds to good risks with credible experience while carrying others at a loss.[8]

Blue Cross and Blue Shield plans show only slightly better underwriting results in recent years than those of private carriers.[9] Eighty-three Blue Cross plans in 1959 showed ratios of losses incurred and expenses incurred to earned subscription income of 93.3 per cent and 5.5 per cent respectively. While

[5] Stanley W. Gingery, "A Reinvestigation of Group Hospital Expense Insurance Experience," *Transactions of the Society of Actuaries,* Vol. 12 (1960), p. 571.

[6] A. B. Halverson, "Major Medical—A Reappraisal," address at Group Insurance Forum, Health Insurance Association of America, February 8, 1960.

[7] Gingery, *op. cit.*

[8] Halverson, *op. cit.*

[9] For all Blue Cross and Blue Shield figures cited see the Spectator Company, *Accident Insurance Register,* 1960, pp. 80–85.

all these plans had a combined ratio of 98.8 per cent of losses and expenses to earned premiums, thirty-three of the plans showed a combined ratio over 100 per cent in 1959.

Seventy-three Blue Shield plans in 1959 showed loss and expense ratios of 90.1 per cent and 10.0 per cent respectively. Thirty-one of this seventy-three had a combined ratio over 100 per cent.

Blue Shield plans, in total, show a lower expense rate than those of private carriers, and Blue Cross plans show a substantially lower expense rate. These lower expense rates are due in part to the relationship of the plans to hospitals and doctors, to a limited number of benefit plan variations, and to the absence of premium and most other taxes, except in Tennessee and Mississippi.

Perhaps the most significant thing about Blue Cross and Blue Shield combined ratios is that individual plans are apparently willing and able to take reasonably prompt corrective action when they suffer underwriting losses, if permitted by regulatory authorities. Thirty-four Blue Cross plans had a combined ratio over 100 per cent in 1957, but only seventeen of these had the ratio increase or remain the same in 1958. Of the thirty-three plans over 100 per cent in 1958, only two increased or remained the same in 1959, and neither of these had operated over 100 per cent in 1957.

Blue Shield plans show a similar pattern of corrective action, although thirty-one of seventy-three plans had combined ratios over 100 per cent in 1959. Only one plan operating without an underwriting gain in 1957 increased its combined ratio in both 1958 and 1959, and the increase was very modest: from 100.0 per cent in 1957, to 100.4 per cent in 1958, and to 100.7 per cent in 1959.

ABUSE OF INSURANCE BENEFITS

It is well known in the insurance industry that insurance for medical care benefits increases the use of medical services. Probably more serious to the industry is the tendency of prepayment systems to create ability to pay for these services that might not be present otherwise. Creating ability to pay was in fact the underlying purpose behind the formation of the first system of prepaying medical care. A person with medical reimbursement benefits in force is automatically able to pay for services up to the amount of his applicable insurance benefits.

There is of course much to be said for charging those able to pay so medical care can be provided to all, but many abuses of insurance benefits are only indirectly related to this practice. Some of the more common causes of unnecessary use of insurance are: (1) the practice of caring for charity patients at less than cost and adding the difference to the private or insured patient's bill, (2) the tendency of doctors to hospitalize and extend the hospitalization period of insured patients as a matter of convenience, and (3) the practice of applying charges to utilize insurance benefits.

The problem of increased charges when the patient is insured is a particularly serious one, and the presence of insurance may not by any means reflect the patient's ability to pay. Doctors are understandably jealous of their rights to set the fees for their services, and they are inclined to feel that such fees are reasonable even if the fee for a given service varies from one doctor to another or even from one patient to another.[10] The problem is more acute in major or comprehensive medical when benefits are not scheduled, and many feel that the "necessary and reasonable" restriction on covered medical expenses is effective only for gross overcharges.[11] Many companies find it necessary to schedule some categories of major and comprehensive medical benefits to give them some claims control. Others, in attempting to restrict coverage to "customary and reasonable" charges, have developed a definition of an "unreasonable" charge as one over the policy relative value schedule, unless the claimant can submit proof of its reasonableness.[12]

---

[10] Halverson, *op. cit.*

[11] Discussion by E. Paul Barnhart, *Transactions of the Society of Actuaries,* Vol. 11 (1959), p. 1041.

[12] Discussion by George N. Watson, *loc. cit.,* p. 487.

Well-known is the general attitude of insured individuals that benefits have been purchased and should therefore be used at every opportunity, without regard for the ultimate effect on premium rates. General check-ups and long hospital stays for rest and convenience are common, especially when the patient is overinsured; and individual doctors and hospitals cannot actively oppose such practices without losing patients.

Many major or comprehensive plans are being revised to reduce or remove areas of full coverage,[13] in an attempt to reduce abuses of the plans from claimants' attitudes. Many companies are changing such plans to scheduled coverage, although there is considerable feeling that doctors are inclined to feel that schedules constitute meddling in the doctor-patient relationship.[14]

The practice of charging higher fees to insured patients effects a fairly widespread application of insurance benefits to the general population, but only the insured pay the costs of these general benefits. The principal objection to this is that there is no organized system of distributing either benefits or costs. A second objection is that abuse of insurance benefits inflates the costs of medical care.

As indicated in Chapter X, substantial progress has been made toward closer co-operation between doctors, hospitals, and all types of insurance carriers in recognizing the serious problems facing medical care insurance. Solving the problem of abuse seems imperative, particularly in view of the increasing interest in major and comprehensive medical insurance. Only by the closest co-operation can such plans provide blanket coverage without detailed scheduling of benefits.

OVERINSURANCE

Overinsurance represents a serious source of abuse of insurance benefits, in that the claimant has a financial incentive to

---

[13] Discussion by Joseph W. Moran, *Transactions of the Society of Actuaries,* Vol. 11 (1959), p. 205.

[14] Discussion by James B. Ross and William Cunningham, *Transactions of the Society of Actuaries,* Vol. 10 (1958), pp. 496–501.

increase his expenditures for medical care or to prolong a disability period. In the field of income reimbursement insurance, overinsurance may result from overlapping of one or more of the following: (1) group insurance, (2) individual insurance, (3) workmen's compensation benefits, (4) federal OASDI benefits, (5) railroad retirement benefits, (6) pension plan disability benefits, (7) automobile policy accident benefits, and (8) liability insurance recoveries.

The problem of duplication of coverage in short-term income reinbursement insurance generally has not been considered as serious, because benefits are ordinarily kept well below take-home pay, and benefit periods are short. In long-term coverage, the problem can be potentially serious, although most companies are very cautious in underwriting practices. Many long-term plans provide that benefits under the plan are to be reduced by any other group insurance benefits, any pension plan disability benefits, and any state or federal plan benefits.[15] Under present laws and regulations generally, companies are not permitted to reduce group insurance benefits because of individual contracts.[16]

The prorating and relation to earnings clauses of individual contracts do provide claims departments with a tool to use in cases involving duplications of group and individual insurance. However, this tool is most useful for obvious overinsurance, because the claimant may not disclose the presence of other insurance.[17] At best it would be an expensive procedure to investigate for duplications of coverage in all cases or even suspicious ones.

Overinsurance in income reimbursement may also arise without duplication of coverage, if wages of insured individuals fall and there is no reduction in insurance benefits. This is

---

[15] Discussion by L. C. Cocheu, Jr., R. D. Albright, and H. F. Harrigan, *Transactions of the Society of Actuaries,* Vol. 10 (1958), pp. 745–48.

[16] Joseph V. McCarthy, "Overinsurance Dangers—Panel Discussion," Health Insurance Association of America, November 17, 1959.

[17] Howard LeClair, "Overinsurance Dangers—Panel Discussion," Health Insurance Association of America, November 17, 1959.

recognized as a serious problem in the long-term income reimbursement field, and underwriting caution appears to be the only answer until such time as a relation-to-earnings provision might be used in group insurance.

Overinsurance in the expense reimbursement field arises only from duplications of coverage, unless full-coverage areas not deterring the claimant from excessive use of his insurance are considered overinsurance. Duplications in coverage in this field may result from the overlapping of one or more of the following: (1) group insurance, (2) individual insurance, (3) liability insurance recoveries, and (4) automobile and other types of medical payments benefits under some policies.

It is fairly simple for an insurer to avoid two group insurance plans provided through a single employer or other policyholder. Duplications of group plans thus will usually arise only when a husband and wife are employed by different employers and both are eligible for group insurance for themselves and their dependents. Most major medical plans today include a nonduplication provision with respect to other group insurance plans.[18] These provisions usually state that the deductible under the plan is to be increased by any benefits payable by a plan toward the cost of which any employer or union makes a contribution or any employer makes a payroll deduction. Such provisions could of course lead to a situation in which persons insured by two plans would be eligible for benefits under neither. In situations such as this, the plans will need to pay on a pro rata basis or the entire industry will need to agree on a primary-secondary relationship of the plans.

Avoiding duplications of group insurance and individual coverage presents the same problems as those discussed above for income reimbursement coverage. Compound duplications of coverage with liability and medical payments insurance have been partially reduced in some states in the automobile insurance field by the Special Automobile Policy. This policy

---

[18] Discussion by Morton D. Miller and G. W. Fitzhugh, *Transactions of the Society of Actuaries,* Vol. 10 (1958), pp. 272–74.

removes at least the duplications of automobile medical payments benefits and other forms of insurance, although the duplication of liability recoveries by group benefits is not removed.

MEDICAL CARE FOR THE AGED

Perhaps the most serious problem facing voluntary health insurance is providing adequate medical expense reimbursement coverage for persons past the normal retirement age of 65. This is particularly serious when it is realized that medical care is today generally regarded as an individual right comparable with the right to food, shelter, and clothing.[19]

The magnitude of the problem is indicated by the fact that in 1959 over fifteen million persons in the United States were over age 65, and this number is expected to reach almost twenty-two million by 1975.[20] In 1940 the over-65 group represented only 6.8 per cent of total United States population, but this group constituted 8.7 per cent of total population in 1959 and might be as much as 9.7 per cent of total by 1975.[21]

The problem of insuring persons to reach age 65 in the future is not the same as that of insuring those already past this age. For those already retired, benefits can be provided through individual insurance, group insurance, or government subsidy. As indicated in Chapter X, voluntary health insurance is making a concerted effort to bring individual coverage to those not easily reached through the ordinary channels of group insurance. A few companies have pioneered in this drive by offering a basic hospital expense policy and guaranteeing its issue to all applicants over age 65 who apply during a stated enrollment period.[22]

---

[19] Mortimer Spiegelman, *Ensuring Medical Care for the Aged* (Homewood, Ill.: Richard D. Irwin, Inc., 1960), p. 237.

[20] *Ibid.*, p. 5.

[21] *Ibid.*

[22] Louis C. Morrell, "What the Senior Citizen Has Meant to Us," Symposium on the Senior Citizen, Health Insurance Association of America, October 24, 1960.

Many persons now over age 65 are insured by converted group coverage or continuation of group insurance after retirement. In addition, group insurance is being extended to persons already retired where these persons can be reached through an association. The two largest groups of this type provided with group insurance are the National Association of Retired Teachers and the National Association of Retired Civil Employees.[23] Retired federal employees are now eligible for coverage under the federal plans, which were discussed in Chapter IV.

As indicated in Chapter IV, there has been much legislative interest in medical care for those past retirement age, and Congress made additional grants-in-aid for this purpose in 1960. This aid is aimed at the older citizens without other means for securing medical care, and these perhaps cannot be reached by any form of voluntary insurance.

Persons not yet retired can be provided with medical expense reimbursement benefits through conversion of group insurance, continuance of group insurance after retirement, or some form of government plan. The progress being made by voluntary insurance in this direction is substantial, and company activities in this area were discussed in Chapter X.

Whether the federal government should provide medical care for the aged is a much debated question of public policy. Many believe such a system would be largely a matter of subsidizing one segment of the population at the expense of the others. This would logically lead to political pressures to extend a government system to all segments of the population.

Even after ten years of operation the British National Health Service is reported to have fallen far short of its goals in providing medical care for the aged.[24] The inadequacy of care for the aged under the British system is generally attributed to an inadequacy of medical facilities.

This same inadequacy of facilities exists in the United States,

---

[23] *Ibid.*
[24] Spiegelman, *op. cit.,* p. 252.

according to the following statement from a report by the Secretary of Health, Education, and Welfare:[25]

There has been and continues to be a serious shortage not only of physicians but also of all other types of health personnel—nurses, occupational and physical therapists, medical and psychiatric social workers, medical technologists, dieticians, and also practical nurses, aides, technicians, and homemakers.

A sudden expansion of coverage entitlement would place an additional burden on medical facilities already in short supply, and this would be true whether the expansion comes from a government system or growth of voluntary insurance. The effect would no doubt be more severe under a government system, because voluntary insurance expansion would be more gradual. Under either type of expansion, however, there will be more inflationary pressure on the costs of medical care unless the availability of medical facilities keeps pace with the growing population and entitlement to medical care.

There is no magic in any system of health insurance, either public or private, which will make medical facilities available at precisely the time they are needed. In fact, a government system of health insurance might well discourage young persons from entering the medical profession. Perhaps government can make a greater contribution to medical care for the aged by concentrating on providing facilities, while voluntary insurance concentrates on an orderly and private system of spreading the costs of using such facilities.

[25] *Hospitalization Insurance for OASDI Beneficiaries,* report to the Committee on Ways and Means, Washington, D.C., April 3, 1959, p. 34.

MODEL GROUP ACCIDENT AND SICKNESS INSURANCE BILL, AS RECOMMENDED BY THE HEALTH INSURANCE ASSOCIATION OF AMERICA, OCTOBER 4, 1957

a. Group accident and sickness insurance is hereby declared to be that form of accident and sickness insurance covering groups of persons as defined below, with or without one or more members of their families or one or more of their dependents, or covering one or more members of the families or one or more dependents of such groups of persons, and issued upon the following basis:

1. Under a policy issued to an employer or trustees of a fund established by an employer, who shall be deemed the policyholder, insuring employees of such employer for the benefit of persons other than the employer. The term "employees" as used herein shall be deemed to include the officers, managers, and employees of the employer, the individual proprietor or partner, if the employer is an individual proprietor or partnership, the officers, managers, and employees of subsidiary or affiliated corporations, the individual proprietors, partners and employees of individuals and firms, if the business of the employer and such individual or firm is under common control through stock ownership, contract, or otherwise. The term "employees" as used herein may include retired employees. A policy issued to insure employees of a public body may provide that the term "employees" shall include elected or appointed officials. The policy may provide that the term "employees"

shall include the trustees or their employees, or both, if their duties are principally connected with such trusteeship.

2. Under a policy issued to an association, including a labor union, which shall have a constitution and bylaws and which has been organized and is maintained in good faith for purposes other than that of obtaining insurance, insuring members, employees, or employees of members of the association for the benefit of persons other than the association or its officers or trustees. The term "employees" as used herein may include retired employees.

3. Under a policy issued to the trustees of a fund established by two or more employers in the same or related industry or by one or more labor unions or by one or more employers and one or more labor unions or by an association as defined in *a*.2, which trustees shall be deemed the policyholder, to insure employees of the employers or members of the unions or of such association, or employees of members of such association for the benefit of persons other than the employers or the unions or such association. The term "employees" as used herein may include the officers, managers, and employees of the employer, and the individual proprietor and partners if the employer is an individual proprietor or partnership. The term "employees" as used herein may include retired employees. The policy may provide that the term "employees" shall include the trustees or their employees, or both, if their duties are principally connected with such trusteeship.

4. Under a policy issued to any person or organization to which a policy of group life insurance may be issued or delivered in this (state) to insure any class or classes of individuals that could be insured under such group life policy.

5. Under a policy issued to cover any other substantially similar group which, in the discretion of the commissioner, may be subject to the issuance of a group accident and sickness policy or contract.

b. Each such policy shall contain in substance the following provisions:

1. A provision that, in the absence of fraud, all statements

made by applicants or the policyholder or by an insured person shall be deemed representations and not warranties, and that no statement made for the purpose of effecting insurance shall avoid such insurance or reduce benefits unless contained in a written instrument signed by the policyholder or the insured person, a copy of which has been furnished to such policyholder or to such person or his beneficiary.

2. A provision that the insurer will furnish to the policyholder for delivery to each employee or member of the insured group, a statement in summary form of the essential features of the insurance coverage of such employee or member and to whom benefits thereunder are payable. If dependents are included in the coverage, only one statement need be issued for each family unit.

3. A provision that to the group originally insured may be added from time to time eligible new employees or members or dependents, as the case may be, in accordance with the terms of the policy.

c. Any group accident and sickness policy may on request by the group policyholder provide that all or any portion of any indemnities provided by any such policy on account of hospital, nursing, medical, or surgical services may, at the insurer's option, be paid directly to the hospital or person rendering such services; but the policy may not require that the service be rendered by a particular hospital or person. Payment so made shall discharge the insurer's obligation with respect to the amount of insurance so paid.

GROUP HEALTH INSURANCE LAWS AND
RULINGS IN EFFECT JANUARY 1, 1961

State	Policy Filing Required	Rate Filing Required	Group Law (L), Ruling (R), or Neither (N)	Minimum Number, Employer Groups	Underwriting Requirements Prescribed for Employer Groups	Underwriting Requirements Prescribed for Other Groups	Some Standard Policy Provisions Required
Alabama	Yes	Yes	N	—	—	—	No
Alaska	Yes	No	N	—	—	—	No
Arizona	Yes	No	L	5	No	No	Yes
Arkansas	Yes	No	L	—	No	No	Yes
California	Yes	No	L	10	No	Yes	Yes
Colorado	Yes	Yes	L	10	No	No	Yes
Connecticut	Yes	No	N	—	—	—	No
Delaware	No	No	N	—	—	—	No
Dist. of Col.	No	No	N	—	—	—	No
Florida	Yes	Yes	L	15	Yes	Yes	Yes
Georgia	Yes	No	L	5	No	No	Yes
Hawaii	No	No	L	—	No	No	Yes
Idaho	No	No	L	—	No	No	Yes
Illinois	Yes	No	L	10	No	No	Yes
Indiana	Yes	Yes	L	10	Yes	Yes	Yes
Iowa	Yes	No	L	10	Yes	Yes	Yes
Kansas	Yes	No	L	5	No	No	Yes
Kentucky	Yes	No	L	—	No	No	Yes
Louisiana	Yes	Yes	L	10	Yes	Yes	Yes
Maine	Yes	Yes	L	10	Yes	Yes	Yes
Maryland	Yes	Yes	R	10	Yes	Yes	No
Massachusetts	No	No	L	—	Yes	Yes	No
Michigan	Yes	Yes	L	5	No	No	Yes
Minnesota	Yes	Yes	L	2	No	No	Yes
Mississippi	Yes	Yes	N	—	—	—	No
Missouri	Yes	No	N	—	—	—	No
Montana	Yes	No	L	—	No	No	Yes
Nebraska	Yes	Yes	L	5	No	No	Yes
Nevada	Yes	No	L	5	No	No	Yes
New Hampshire	Yes	Yes	N	—	—	—	Yes
New Jersey	Yes	No	L	2	No	No	Yes
New Mexico	Yes	Yes	L	10	No	No	Yes
New York	Yes	Yes	L	2	Yes	Yes	Yes
North Carolina	Yes	Yes	L	2	Yes	Yes	Yes
North Dakota	Yes	Yes	N	—	—	—	No
Ohio	Yes	Yes	L	10	No	No	Yes
Oklahoma	Yes	Yes	L	10	No	No	Yes
Oregon	Yes	Yes	L	—	No	No	No
Pennsylvania	Yes	No	L	10	No	No	Yes
Rhode Island	Yes	No	N	—	—	—	No
South Carolina	Yes	No	L	10	Yes	Yes	No
South Dakota	No	No	N	—	—	—	No
Tennessee	No	No	N	—	—	—	No
Texas	Yes	No	N	—	—	—	No
Utah	Yes	No	L	10	Yes	Yes	No
Vermont	Yes	Yes	L	5	No	No	Yes
Virginia	Yes	Yes	N	—	—	—	No
Washington	Yes	Yes	L	—	No	No	Yes
West Virginia	Yes	No	L	10	Yes	No	Yes
Wisconsin	Yes	Yes	L	10	No	No	Yes
Wyoming	No	No	N	—	—	—	No

INDEX

This book has been set on the Linotype in 12
point and 10 point Garamond #3, leaded 1
point. Chapter numbers are in 14 point Garamond #248; chapter titles are in 14 point
Lydian Bold. The size of the type page is 24 by
42 picas.